# CONTENTS

1

# MARILYN MONROE: ENCHANTRESS

BY F. X. FEENEY

**MARILYN MONROE: DAS ZAUBERWESEN**

**MARILYN MONROE : L'ENCHANTERESSE**

# MARILYN MONROE: ENCHANTRESS

by F. X. Feeney

"Forget everything you think you know about this person," Elia Kazan cautioned in his autobiography. The icon we cherish under the name Marilyn Monroe was in truth the inspired creation of a smart, voluptuous, star-struck and self-motivated fantasist named Norma Jean Mortenson. A pure product of Hollywood, California, she abides across time as brightly as two other self-inventors, Charlie Chaplin and Cary Grant – if not more so. "Marilyn Monroe" was a name she fashioned herself, in part from the maiden name of a mother she barely knew. When Kazan met her in the late 1940s, she was still going privately by the name Norma Jean, still playing inconsequential bit parts in a variety of movies for 20th Century-Fox. She had by then survived a hard luck childhood in orphanages and foster homes, and the sudden death of her one reliable protector, agent Johnny Hyde. Her sexy optimism so impressed Kazan that, after an affair with her of his own, he introduced her to playwright Arthur Miller – whom she eventually married.

Marilyn's unique radiance is self-evident in nearly every photo ever taken of her. She projected her sexuality freely – and this freedom, so lightly defiant of traditional inhibitions, made her mass appeal inevitable. Her exceptional openness, her aura of complete availability, made sex feel like a healthy idea – the last thing in the world any sane person would repress. The titles of her first star vehicles in the early 1950s milk this with a lusty exuberance: *As Young as You Feel, Love Nest, Let's Make It Legal, Clash by Night, We're Not Married, Don't Bother to Knock, Monkey Business*. Her 'blonde bombshell' persona was so vivid that, like Chaplin before her, she launched a myriad of imitators. But as she was infinitely more ambitious than those who copied her (and in this she was like Chaplin, too), Marilyn fought free of what she'd pioneered and surprised fans by demanding roles of increasing dignity and complexity. After she made *The Seven Year Itch* in 1955, she formed Marilyn Monroe Productions, studied acting

**PORTRAIT (1950)**
A siren-in-waiting, posed à la Jean Harlow. / Eine lauernde Sirene in Jean-Harlow-Pose. / Une sirène rêveuse, posant à la Jean Harlow.

"A sex-symbol becomes a thing, I just hate being a thing. But if I'm going to be a symbol of something I'd rather have it sex than some other things we've got symbols of."
Marilyn Monroe

with Lee Strasberg at the Actors Studio, and married Arthur Miller. Cynics mocked her eagerness to be taken seriously, but she brushed these detractors aside.

Miller had a sensitive insight into her mastery of what he called 'the orphan's anthem, charm.' He saw clearly the still-open (if well-hidden) wound that both powered her rise and threatened to destroy her. 'She had wanted everything, but one thing contradicted another,' Miller would write in his memoirs: 'Physical admiration threatened to devalue her person, yet she became anxious if her appearance was ignored.' Over the five years of their marriage, Miller grew alarmed at her increasing dependency on both sleeping pills and the counsel of her teachers, Lee and Paula Strasberg. He feared the pills were endangering her life, and that the cultish Strasberg "method" was crippling her as an artist. Marilyn nevertheless made the films for which she is now most substantially remembered, in her time with Miller – *Bus Stop* (one of her most layered performances, from a script by William Inge), *The Prince and the Showgirl* (opposite Laurence Olivier, who also directed her), *Some Like It Hot* (where she quarreled with Billy Wilder but blazes delightfully), and, above all, *The Misfits*, where she battled and divorced Miller – who wrote it for her. Despite their private ordeals, the film certainly makes visible the Marilyn *he* loved.

She sang at President John F. Kennedy's 1962 birthday gala two months before her death. This coincidence has since inspired an oceanic orgy of pornographic fantasy linking her tragic fate to those of the Kennedys. (Buyer, beware: Monroe and JFK were both light and expert in matters of sexual adventure, and their paths certainly crossed, but there is no hard evidence of any continuous or significant relationship more than a one-night stand between them.) Marilyn was nevertheless in a deep crisis that summer. None of her marriages had worked out. Her chronic oversleeping, lateness, and twin dependencies on pills and reassurance got her fired from a mostly complete film, *Something's Got to Give* – though after four weeks of wrangling, these differences were agreeably settled. Marilyn signed a fresh contract to finish the picture on even more advantageous financial terms than before, and made plans to travel to New York. The police found no note by her bedside when they discovered her dead of a barbiturate overdose a mere four days later, in the early hours of 5 August 1962. For all the mythology that has surrounded her last night on earth, the simplest explanation is likeliest – that with her daily, often round-the-clock pill intake, Marilyn lost track of her dosage and, after years of risking this, drowned in Dreamland.

Few things make an afterlife blaze more mythically than a sexual reputation. Norma Jean paid a huge price, becoming Marilyn, yet here she is – still with us, still charming and enchanting us, still setting the bar high for all other would-be goddesses.

**PORTRAIT FOR 'ALL ABOUT EVE' (1950)**
The young starlet in a classy role. / Das junge Starlet in einer Rolle mit Klasse. / La jeune starlette dans un rôle chic.

# MARILYN MONROE: DAS ZAUBERWESEN

von F. X. Feeney

„Vergessen Sie alles, was Sie über diesen Menschen zu wissen glauben", mahnte Elia Kazan die Leser seiner Autobiografie. Die Ikone, die wir unter dem Namen Marilyn Monroe verehren, war in Wahrheit die geniale Schöpfung einer sinnlichen, klugen, zielstrebigen Träumerin namens Norma Jean Mortenson, die von Prominenz geblendet war. Als reines Hollywood-Produkt hat sie die Zeiten genauso gut überdauert wie zwei andere Ikonen von eigenen Gnaden: Charlie Chaplin und Cary Grant – vielleicht sogar besser. „Marilyn Monroe" war ein Name, den sie sich selbst ausgedacht hatte, und zwar nach dem Mädchennamen ihrer Mutter, die sie kaum kannte. Als Kazan sie Ende der vierziger Jahre des letzten Jahrhunderts kennenlernte, benutzte sie privat noch immer den Namen Norma Jean und spielte belanglose Röllchen in verschiedenen Filmen für 20th Century-Fox. Zu diesem Zeitpunkt lag bereits eine harte Kindheit in Waisenhäusern und Pflegefamilien hinter ihr, und vor allem hatte sie da schon den plötzlichen Tod ihres einzigen verlässlichen Beschützers, des Agenten Johnny Hyde, verkraften müssen. Kazan war von ihrer sinnlichen Lebenslust so beeindruckt, dass er sich erst selbst auf eine Affäre mit ihr einließ und sie anschließend dem Dramatiker Arthur Miller vorstellte, den sie schließlich heiratete.

Marilyns einzigartige Ausstrahlung fällt in fast jedem Foto, das jemals von ihr gemacht wurde, sofort ins Auge. Sie stellte ihre Sexualität freizügig zur Schau – und diese Freiheit, die sich so leichtfüßig über traditionelle Hemmungen hinwegsetzte, machte sie unweigerlich zu einem Idol der Massen. Durch ihre außergewöhnliche Offenheit und den Anschein, von Kopf bis Fuß verfügbar zu sein, erschien sexuelles Begehren als etwas Gesundes, das kein Mensch bei klarem Verstand jemals unterdrücken würde. Die Originaltitel ihrer ersten Filme aus den frühen fünfziger Jahren, in denen sie Hauptrollen hatte, spielen denn auch mit unverhohlener Lüsternheit auf diese Vorstellungen an: *Alter schützt vor Torheit nicht*, *Love Nest*, *Let's Make It Legal*, *Vor dem neuen Tag*, *Wir sind gar nicht verheiratet*, *Versuchung auf 809*, *Liebling, ich werde jünger*. Ihr Bild als „blonde Sexbombe" war so lebendig, dass sie (wie Chaplin vor ihr) unzählige Nachahmer auf den Plan rief. Weil sie aber so unendlich viel ehrgeiziger war als ihre Imitatoren (und auch darin glich sie Chaplin), konnte sich Marilyn von dem selbst erschaffenen Image befreien und überraschte ihre Fans, indem sie anspruchsvollere und würdevollere Rollen für sich forderte. Nachdem sie 1955 *Das verflixte 7. Jahr* gedreht hatte, gründete sie Marilyn Monroe Productions, studierte unter Lee Strasberg in dessen „Actors Studio" ernsthaft die Schauspielkunst und heiratete Arthur Miller. Zyni-

*„Ein Sexsymbol wird zum Ding, und ich hasse es einfach, ein Ding zu sein. Aber wenn ich ein Symbol für irgendetwas sein soll, dann lieber für Sex als für einige andere Dinge, für die wir Symbole haben."*
**Marilyn Monroe**

**PORTRAIT (c. 1956)**
She was in command of her persona from the very start. / Vom Start weg hatte sie ihre Persona voll im Griff. / Dès ses débuts, elle avait le contrôle de ses propres personnages.

ker spöttelten über ihr Streben, ernstgenommen zu werden, doch sie wies solche Anfechtungen zurück.

Miller begriff mit seinem Einfühlungsvermögen, dass Marilyn es meisterlich verstand, „die Hymne der Waisen, den Charme", spielen zu lassen. Er sah ganz deutlich die noch immer offene (wenn auch gut versteckte) Wunde, die ihren Aufstieg ermöglicht hatte, aber auch ihren Niedergang herbeiführen konnte. „Sie wollte alles haben, aber ihre Ziele widersprachen einander", schrieb Miller in seinen Memoiren: „Die Bewunderung für ihren Körper drohte ihre Person abzuwerten, doch wenn ihr Erscheinungsbild übergangen wurde, war sie beunruhigt." In den fünf Jahren ihrer Ehe machte sich Miller immer mehr Sorgen über ihre wachsende Abhängigkeit von Schlaftabletten einerseits und dem Rat ihrer Lehrer, Lee und Paula Strasberg, andererseits. Er fürchtete, die Tabletten könnten ihr Leben ernsthaft gefährden und die kultartige „Method"-Lehre der Strasbergs könne sie künstlerisch verkrüppeln. Marilyn drehte dennoch jene Filme, derentwegen man sich ihrer heute hauptsächlich erinnert, während ihrer Ehe mit Miller – *Bus Stop* (eine ihrer vielschichtigsten darstellerischen Leistungen), *Der Prinz und die Tänzerin* (neben Laurence Olivier), *Manche mögen's heiß* und vor allem *Misfits – Nicht gesellschaftsfähig*, wo sie sich mit Miller, der ihr das Drehbuch auf den Leib geschrieben hatte, zerstritt und sich scheiden ließ. Trotz ihrer privaten Querelen zeigt der Film sicherlich jene Marilyn, die *er* liebte.

Zwei Monate vor ihrem Tod sang sie 1962 anlässlich der Geburtstagsgala für Präsident John F. Kennedy. Dieser Zufall hat seither eine Flutwelle pornografischer Phantasien ausgelöst, die ihr tragisches Schicksal mit dem der Kennedys verknüpfen. (*Caveat emptor*: Monroe und JFK kannten sich wohl beide mit Affären aus, und ihre Wege haben sich auch gekreuzt, aber es gibt keine greifbaren Indizien für eine bedeutungsvolle und anhaltende Beziehung der beiden, die über einen One-Night-Stand hinausginge.) Marilyn steckte dennoch in jenem Sommer in einer tiefen Krise. Alle ihre Ehen waren gescheitert. Ihr chronisches Verschlafen, ihre Unpünktlichkeit und ihre doppelte Abhängigkeit von Tabletten und persönlicher Bestätigung hatten schließlich zur Folge, dass sie aus einem Film gefeuert wurde, der schon fast fertig war: *Marilyn – Ihr letzter Film* – wenngleich die Differenzen nach vier Wochen zäher Verhandlungen im gegenseitigen Einvernehmen beigelegt wurden. Marilyns neuer Vertrag über die Fertigstellung des Films war finanziell noch lukrativer als ihr alter, und sie plante eine Reise nach New York. Als man sie nur vier Tage später, in den frühen Morgenstunden des 5. August 1962, mit einer Überdosis an Barbituraten tot im Bett fand, konnte die Polizei keinen Abschiedsbrief entdecken. Trotz aller Mythen, die sich um ihre letzte Nacht auf Erden ranken, ist die einfachste Erklärung die wahrscheinlichste: dass Marilyn, die täglich oft rund um die Uhr Pillen schluckte, irgendwann den Überblick über die Dosierung verlor und nach jahrelangem Spiel mit dem Feuer schließlich für immer in das Land der ewigen Träume abtauchte.

Was eignete sich besser, einem Leben nach dem Tod mythische Dimensionen zu verleihen, als eine sexuelle Reputation? Norma Jean zahlte einen hohen Preis dafür, dass sie zu Marilyn wurde, doch hier ist sie – noch immer unter uns, noch immer reizend und bezaubernd, noch immer der Maßstab für alle anderen Möchtegern-Göttinnen.

**PORTRAIT (1953)**
Sexuality personified, and magnified by Hollywood. /
Personifizierte Sexualität im Vergrößerungsglas
Hollywoods. / La sexualité incarnée, magnifiée par
Hollywood.

# MARILYN MONROE : L'ENCHANTERESSE

F. X. Feeney

« Oubliez tout ce que vous pensez savoir sur elle », avertit Elia Kazan dans son autobiographie. L'idole que nous chérissons sous le nom de Marilyn Monroe est en réalité la création inspirée d'une femme intelligente, voluptueuse, ambitieuse et fascinée par la célébrité, appelée Norma Jean Mortenson. En pur produit d'Hollywood, elle a traversé le temps avec autant de fulgurance – si ce n'est davantage – que deux autres grands noms du cinéma également « inventeurs » de leur propre personnage : Charlie Chaplin et Cary Grant. « Marilyn Monroe » est un nom qu'elle a façonné en s'inspirant partiellement du nom de jeune fille d'une mère qu'elle a à peine connue. Lorsque Kazan la rencontre à la fin des années 1940, elle se fait encore appeler Norma Jean en privé et joue des petits rôles inconséquents dans divers films de la 20th Century-Fox. Bien que marquée par une enfance malheureuse passée entre orphelinats et familles d'accueil, ainsi que par la mort brutale de son unique et fidèle protecteur – son agent Johnny Hyde – son optimisme sensuel impressionne tant Kazan qu'il noue une brève relation avec elle avant de lui présenter le dramaturge Arthur Miller, qu'elle finit par épouser.

Le rayonnement unique de Marilyn émane de la quasi-totalité de ses photos. Elle projette librement sa sexualité – et cette liberté, qui provoque de façon si subtile les inhibitions traditionnelles, fait inévitablement succomber le grand public. Son exceptionnelle franchise, sa disponibilité naturelle, donnent l'impression que le sexe est une idée saine – la dernière chose au monde que toute personne saine irait réprimer. Les titres des premiers films ayant contribué à sa notoriété au début des années 1950 le soulignent avec exubérance : *Rendez-moi ma femme, Nid d'amour, Chéri, divorçons, Le démon s'éveille la nuit, Cinq mariages à l'essai, Troublez-moi ce soir, Chéri, je me sens rajeunir*. Son personnage de « bombe blonde » est si éclatant que – comme Chaplin avant elle – elle lance une myriade d'imitatrices. Mais comme elle est infiniment plus ambitieuse que celles qui la copient (ce en quoi elle ressemble aussi beaucoup à Chaplin), Marilyn lutte pour se libérer du carcan qu'elle a créé et surprend ses admirateurs en exigeant des rôles de plus en plus sérieux et complexes. Après *Sept ans de réflexion*, en 1955, elle monte la société Marilyn Monroe Productions, étudie le jeu d'acteur avec Lee Strasberg à l'Actors Studio et épouse Arthur Miller. Certains esprits cyniques tournent en dérision son désir si intense d'être prise au sérieux, mais elle dédaigne ces détracteurs.

**PORTRAIT (c. 1953)**
She later rejected this big studio brand of exaggerated intensity. / Später lehnte sie diese übertriebene Intensität ab, die für die großen Studios typisch war. / Plus tard, elle rejettera cette intensité exagérée qui était la marque des gros studios.

*« Un sex-symbol devient une chose, je déteste être une chose. Mais si je dois vraiment être le symbole de quelque chose, j'aime autant que ce soit du sexe plutôt que d'autres choses pour lesquelles nous avons déjà des symboles. »*
Marilyn Monroe

Miller ressent de manière très sensible sa maîtrise de ce qu'il appelle « le thème de la charmante orpheline ». Il voit clairement la blessure encore ouverte (mais bien cachée) qui est à la fois le moteur de son ascension et le poison menaçant de la détruire. « Elle voulait tout en même temps, mais tout était contradictoire », écrira Miller dans ses mémoires : « L'admiration qu'inspirait son physique menaçait de dévaloriser sa personne, mais elle était angoissée à l'idée que son apparence puisse rester ignorée. » Au cours des cinq années que dure leur mariage, Miller vient à s'inquiéter de sa dépendance toujours croissante tant aux somnifères qu'aux conseils de ses mentors, Lee et Paula Strasberg. Il craint que les pilules ne mettent sa vie en danger et que la « méthode Strasberg » ne l'écrase en tant qu'artiste. Au cours de son mariage avec Miller, Marilyn tourne cependant les films qui la feront entrer dans la légende : *L'Arrêt d'autobus* – un de ses rôles les plus touffus, d'après un scénario de William Inge –, *Le Prince et la danseuse* – face à Laurence Olivier, également à la réalisation –, *Certains l'aiment chaud* – où elle resplendit, malgré ses rapports houleux avec Billy Wilder –, mais aussi *Les Désaxés*, pendant le tournage duquel elle et Miller – qui a écrit le rôle pour elle – se déchirent puis divorcent. Malgré les épreuves que le couple traverse en coulisse, le film montre très certainement le visage de la Marilyn qu'il aimait.

Le tour de chant mémorable qu'elle donne – deux ans avant sa mort – à l'occasion du gala organisé en 1962 pour l'anniversaire du Président John F. Kennedy ne manquera pas d'alimenter les rumeurs et un raz-de-marée de fantasmes indécents, liant ainsi son destin tragique à celui des Kennedy. (Que les choses soient claires : Monroe et JFK considéraient tous deux les choses du sexe avec légèreté – et en experts ! –, et leurs routes se sont certes croisées, mais il n'existe aucune preuve concrète d'une quelconque relation suivie ou sérieuse qui aurait dépassé le stade de la passade.) Il n'en est pas moins vrai que Marilyn traverse cet été-là une crise profonde. Aucun de ses mariages n'a fonctionné. Ses pannes d'oreiller chroniques, ses retards, et sa double dépendance aux médicaments et au réconfort provoquent son renvoi du plateau de *Something's Got to Give* à quelques jours seulement de la fin du tournage ; mais après quatre semaines de tractations, le différend trouve un dénouement heureux. Marilyn signe un tout nouveau contrat pour finir le film selon des termes encore plus avantageux financièrement et prévoit de partir en voyage à New York. La police ne trouve aucun mot à côté de son lit lorsque, quatre jours plus tard – aux premières heures du 5 août 1962 –, elle découvre le corps sans vie de Marilyn, emportée par une overdose de barbituriques. Une mythologie foisonnante entoure sa dernière nuit sur Terre, mais l'explication la plus simple est aussi la plus probable : avec la quantité de médicaments qu'elle avalait tout au long de la journée, Marilyn avait fini par perdre pied dans le monde ici-bas pour sombrer dans le Pays des rêves qui l'attirait à lui depuis tant d'années.

Peu de choses rendent un mythe posthume plus glorieux qu'une réputation de sensualité débridée. Norma Jean a payé un prix faramineux, en devenant Marilyn, et pourtant elle est toujours à nos côtés – toujours enjôleuse et ravissante, damant encore le pion aux apprenties déesses.

**PORTRAIT (1958)**
Celebrating the start of production on 'Some Like It Hot.' / Der Beginn der Dreharbeiten zu *Manche mögen's heiß* wird gefeiert. / Fêtant le lancement du tournage de *Certains l'aiment chaud.*

# 2

# VISUAL
# FILMOGRAPHY

## FILMOGRAFIE IN BILDERN
## FILMOGRAPHIE EN IMAGES

# BACKGROUND
# BLONDE

## BLONDINE IM HINTERGRUND

## UNE SILHOUETTE BLONDE

"As I grew older I knew I was different from the other girls because there were no kisses or promises in my life. I often felt lonely and wanted to die."
Marilyn Monroe, 'My Story'

„Als ich älter wurde, wusste ich, dass ich anders war als die anderen Mädchen, weil es in meinem Leben keine Küsse oder Versprechen gab.
Ich fühlte mich oft einsam und wollte sterben."
Marilyn Monroe, My Story

« En grandissant, j'ai compris que j'étais différente des autres filles parce que je n'avais connu ni baisers ni promesses au cours de ma vie. Souvent, je me sentais seule et je voulais mourir. »
Marilyn Monroe, My Story

PAGE 22
**PORTRAIT (c. 1947)**
She was still Norma Jean, and a woman who could only be noticed. / Sie war noch immer Norma Jean und eine Frau, die man nicht übersehen konnte. / Norma Jean, une femme qui ne pouvait qu'être remarquée avant même de devenir Marilyn.

PAGES 26/27
**PORTRAIT FOR 'LADIES OF THE CHORUS' (1948)**
Studiously exercising for the camera. / Fleißig übt sie für die Kamera. / S'exerçant studieusement face à la caméra.

**PORTRAIT (c. 1947)**
Who knew the early American Puritans were this fetching? / Wer hätte gedacht, dass die frühen Puritaner in Amerika so attraktiv waren? / Qui eût cru que les Puritains américains pouvaient être si séduisants ?

**PORTRAITS (c. 1948)**
Making a little extra money by modeling how to apply
make-up. / Sie zeigt anderen, wie man Make-up richtig
aufträgt, und verdient sich damit ein kleines Zubrot. /
Marilyn arrondit les fins de mois en servant de
mannequin pour des leçons de maquillage.

**PORTRAIT (1950)**
"The camera loved her," as the saying goes, and it was mutual. / „Die Kamera liebte sie", heißt es - eine Liebe auf Gegenseitigkeit. / « La caméra l'adorait », comme on l'entend souvent, et elle le lui rendait bien.

*"My impulse to appear naked and my dreams about it had no shame or sense of sin in them. Dreaming of people looking at me made me feel less lonely."*
**Marilyn Monroe, 'My Story'**

**PORTRAIT (1951)**
Few have ever offered themselves so freely or fully to the lens. / Nur wenige gaben sich je so frei und mit Haut und Haar der Kamera hin. / Peu d'actrices se sont offertes plus librement et totalement à l'objectif.

„Mein Antrieb, mich nackt zu zeigen, und meine Träume davon hatten nichts Schamhaftes oder Sündiges. Ich fühlte mich weniger einsam, wenn ich davon träumte, dass mich Leute anschauten."
Marilyn Monroe, *My Story*

« Mon envie d'apparaître nue et les rêves que j'ai faits à ce propos ne comportaient aucun sentiment de honte ou de péché. Rêver de gens qui me regardaient me permettait de me sentir moins seule. »
Marilyn Monroe, *My Story*

**STILL FROM 'DANGEROUS YEARS' (1947)**
Her first film role, a bit part, opposite William
Hallop. / Ihre erste Filmrolle war ein Miniauftritt an
der Seite von William Hallop. / Son premier rôle de
cinéma, une apparition face à William Hallop.

*"I used to think as I looked at the Hollywood night,
'There must be thousands of girls sitting alone like
me, dreaming of becoming a movie star. But I'm not
going to worry about them. I'm dreaming the
hardest.'"*
**Marilyn Monroe**

*„Wenn ich nachts auf Hollywood schaute, dann
dachte ich immer: ,Da draußen müssen Tausende
von Mädchen sitzen, die genauso einsam sind wie
ich und davon träumen, ein Filmstar zu werden.
Aber über die mache ich mir keine Gedanken.
Ich träume einfach am festesten.'"*
**Marilyn Monroe**

**STILL FROM 'SCUDDA HOO! SCUDDA HAY!'
(1948)**
The uncredited Girl in the Boat with Robert Karnes
and Colleen Townsend. / Als ungenannte Statistin mit
Robert Karnes und Colleen Townsend (im Boot, hinten). / La scène coupée au montage de la Fille dans la
barque, avec Robert Karnes et Colleen Townsend. Le
nom de Marilyn Monroe n'apparaît pas au générique.

*« Avant, je regardais la nuit au-dessus de
Hollywood et je me disais : "Il doit y avoir des
milliers de filles assises toutes seules comme moi,
à rêver qu'elles deviendront des stars du cinéma.
Mais je ne vais pas me préoccuper d'elles.
C'est moi qui rêve le plus fort." »*
Marilyn Monroe

**STILL FROM 'LADIES OF THE CHORUS' (1948)**
Standing out from the crowd, with a bit of help
from the costumer. / Sie hebt sich von der Masse
ab – mit ein wenig Schützenhilfe vom Kostümbildner. /
Sous les feux de la rampe, sublimée par un costume à
la mesure de son talent.

**STILL FROM 'LADIES OF THE CHORUS' (1948)**
As a showgirl being courted by a wealthy beau. /
Als Showgirl, dem ein wohlhabender Stutzer den Hof
macht. / En danseuse courtisée par un riche bellâtre.

**STILL FROM 'LOVE HAPPY' (1950)**
Marilyn supplies the only life, besides Groucho Marx, in this dull film. / Marilyn ist neben Groucho Marx das einzig Lebendige in diesem Langweiler. / Marilyn est la seule, en dehors de Groucho Marx, à insuffler de la vie à ce film ennuyeux.

**Marilyn:** *"Some men are following me."*
**Groucho:** *"Really? I can't understand why."*

**Klientin (Monroe):** *„Ich werde von einigen Männern verfolgt."*
**Sam Grunion (Groucho Marx):** *„Wirklich? Das kann ich gar nicht verstehen."*

**Marilyn.** *– Des hommes me suivent.*
**Groucho.** *– Vraiment ? Je me demande bien pourquoi.*

**ON THE SET OF 'LOVE HAPPY' (1950)**
Groucho only made the film to help his brother Chico
out of debt. / Groucho drehte diesen Film nur, um
seinem verschuldeten Bruder Chico zu helfen. /
Groucho n'a fait ce film que pour aider son frère Chico
à rembourser ses dettes.

*"Mae West, Theda Bara and Bo Peep rolled into
one."*
**Groucho Marx**

*„Mae West, Theda Bara und Bo Peep in einer
Person."*
**Groucho Marx**

*« [Marilyn, c'est] Mae West, Theda Bara et Bo
Peep roulées en une seule personne. »*
**Groucho Marx**

**STILL FROM 'A TICKET TO TOMAHAWK'
(1950)**
The story centers on a race between a stagecoach and a locomotive. / Die Geschichte handelt von einem Wettrennen zwischen einer Postkutsche und einer Lokomotive. / L'histoire tourne autour d'une course entre une diligence et une locomotive.

**PAGES 40 & 41
ON THE SET OF & STILL FROM
'THE ASPHALT JUNGLE' (1950)**
Her first substantial role, as the "niece" (read mistress) of crooked Louis Calhern (left). / Ihre erste bedeutende Rolle als „Nichte" (sprich Geliebte) des betrügerischen Hehlers (Louis Calhern, links). / Sur le plateau pour son premier rôle substantiel : celui de la « nièce » (comprenez « maîtresse ») de l'escroc interprété par Louis Calhern (à gauche).

**STILL FROM 'A TICKET TO TOMAHAWK'
(1950)**
Executing a dance step with soft-shoe expert, Dan Dailey. / Marilyn beim Steptanz mit Dan Dailey, einem Meister des Soft-Shoe-Tanzes. / Exécutant un pas de danse avec le roi des claquettes sans fers, Dan Dailey.

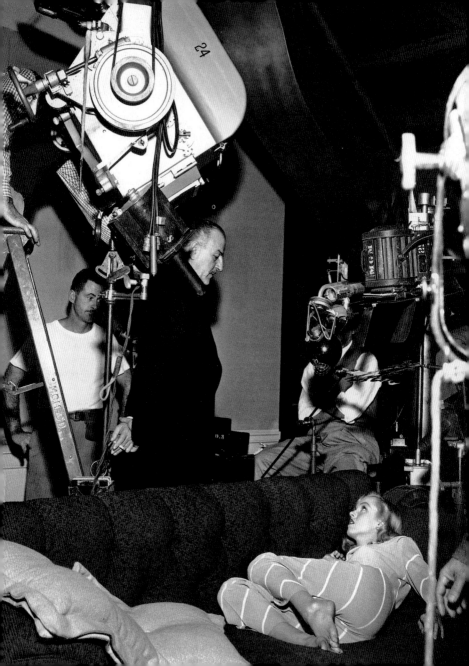

**STILL FROM 'THE ASPHALT JUNGLE' (1950)**
At a key moment, she betrays Calhern to a detective
(Pat Flaherty). / In einer Schlüsselszene verrät sie Lon
(Calhern) an einen Polizisten (Pat Flaherty). / À un
moment décisif, elle dénonce Calhern à un policier
(Pat Flaherty).

**PORTRAIT FOR 'THE ASPHALT JUNGLE'
(1950)**
"I cast her because she was so damn good," said
director John Huston. / „Die Rolle bekam sie, weil sie
so verdammt gut war", sagte Regisseur John Huston. /
« Je l'ai engagée parce qu'elle était sacrément
bonne », confia le réalisateur John Huston.

**STILL FROM 'ALL ABOUT EVE' (1950)**
A small but showy role, opposite Bette Davis and
George Sanders. / Eine kleine, aber auffällige Rolle
neben Bette Davis und George Sanders. / Dans un rôle
modeste mais tape-à-l'œil, face à Bette Davis et
George Sanders.

*"My illusions didn't have anything to do with being
a fine actress. I knew how third rate I was. I could
actually feel my lack of talent, as if it were cheap
clothes I was wearing inside. But my God, how
I wanted to learn, to change, to improve!"*
Marilyn Monroe

*„Meine Illusionen hatten nichts damit zu tun,
eine gute Schauspielerin zu sein. Ich wusste,
wie drittklassig ich war. Ich konnte meinen
Talentmangel richtig spüren, wie billige Kleider, die
ich in meinem Inneren trug. Aber, mein Gott, ich
wollte lernen, mich ändern, mich verbessern!"*
Marilyn Monroe

**STILL FROM 'THE FIREBALL' (1950)**
Mickey Rooney (right) was the star, Marilyn a mere
accessory. / Mickey Rooney (rechts) war der Star,
Marilyn nur eine Zugabe. / Mickey Rooney (à droite)
était la vedette, Marilyn un simple accessoire.

« Mes illusions n'avaient rien à voir avec le fait
d'être une bonne actrice. Je savais à quel point
j'étais médiocre. Je pouvais réellement ressentir
mon manque de talent, comme des vêtements
bas de gamme que j'aurais portés à l'intérieur de
moi. Mais, mon Dieu, comme je voulais apprendre,
changer, m'améliorer ! »
**Marilyn Monroe**

**STILL FROM 'RIGHT CROSS' (1950)**
Dick Powell played a sportswriter. Marilyn was
uncredited. / Dick Powell spielte einen
Sportjournalisten. Marilyn wurde nicht genannt. /
Dick Powell en journaliste sportif. Marilyn n'est pas
créditée.

"Nobody discovered her. She earned her own way
to stardom."
Darryl Zanuck

„Sie wurde von niemandem entdeckt. Sie hat sich
selbst zum Star hochgearbeitet."
Darryl Zanuck

« Personne ne l'a découverte. Elle a pavé
elle-même le chemin qui l'a menée vers la
célébrité. »
Darryl Zanuck

### STILL FROM 'HOME TOWN STORY' (1951)
Alan Hale, Jr. as a newsman, Marilyn cool in her last role for MGM. Notice she is wearing the same top as for 'The Fireball' - it came from her own wardrobe. / Alan Hale jr. als Reporter, Marilyn ganz „cool" in ihrer letzten Rolle für die MGM. Man beachte, dass sie dasselbe Oberteil trägt wie in *Rollschuhfieber* - es stammte aus ihrer eigenen Garderobe. / Alan Hale Jr en journaliste, Marilyn détendue dans son dernier rôle pour la MGM. Notez qu'elle porte le même haut que dans *The Fireball* (garde-robe personnelle).

**STILL FROM 'AS YOUNG AS YOU FEEL' (1951)**
Surprised at a plot twist in this satirical comedy.
With Wally Brown. / Die Handlung nimmt eine
überraschende Wendung in dieser satirischen
Komödie mit Wally Brown. / Frappée de surprise
lors d'un rebondissement de la comédie satirique
dont elle partage l'affiche avec Wally Brown.

**PUBLICITY FOR 'AS YOUNG AS YOU FEEL'
(1951)**
The star climbs her ladder, and looks determined to
stay. / Der Star erklimmt eine Leiter und scheint
entschlossen, oben bleiben zu wollen. / La star gravit
son échelle et semble décidée à y rester.

the whole family to see!
CONSTANCE
BENNETT
MARILYN
MONROE
YOU FE
JONES · SCREEN PLAY BY LAMAR TROTTI 20

**STILL FROM 'LOVE NEST' (1951)**
Squaring off in a comical, territorial battle with June
Haver. / In einem witzigen Gebietskampf mit June
Haver. / Aux prises avec June Haver dans une joute
territoriale désopilante.

*"I want to be a big star more than anything."*
Marilyn Monroe

*„Mehr als alles andere wünsche ich mir, ein großer
Star zu sein."*
Marilyn Monroe

*« Plus que tout, je veux être une grande star. »*
Marilyn Monroe

**STILL FROM 'LET'S MAKE IT LEGAL' (1951)**
MacDonald Carey backs her into Zachary Scott and
Claudette Colbert. / Macdonald Carey verursacht
ihren Zusammenstoß mit Zachary Scott und Claudette
Colbert. / Avec MacDonald Carey, Zachary Scott et
Claudette Colbert.

PAGE 52
**STILL FROM 'CLASH BY NIGHT' (1952)**
Working in a fish cannery, under the direction
of the great Fritz Lang. / Arbeit in einer
Fischkonservenfabrik unter der Regie des großen Fritz
Lang. / Employée dans une conserverie de poissons,
sous la direction du grand Fritz Lang.

# WORKING GIRL

## FLEISSIGES MÄDCHEN

## LES ANNÉES STUDIEUSES

**STILL FROM 'CLASH BY NIGHT' (1952)**
Swept merrily off her feet by Keith Andes. /
Von Keith Andes ist sie offenbar ganz
hingerissen. / Littéralement renversée par
Keith Andes.

**STILL FROM 'CLASH BY NIGHT' (1952)**
Andes is her husband in this superb drama. / Andes
spielt in diesem herausragenden Drama ihren
Ehemann. / Andes joue son époux dans ce drame
sublime.

**STILL FROM 'CLASH BY NIGHT' (1952)**
Writer Alfred Hayes, adapting Clifford Odets, created layered tensions. / Nach einer Vorlage von Clifford Odets schuf Drehbuchautor Alfred Hayes Spannung auf mehreren Ebenen. / Alfred Hayes, qui adapte le texte de Clifford Odets, réussit à créer une tension particulièrement dense.

**STILL FROM 'CLASH BY NIGHT' (1952)**
A complex image of love and mistrust, typical of director Fritz Lang. / Ein komplexes Bild von Liebe und Misstrauen, typisch für den Regisseur Fritz Lang. / Une représentation complexe de l'amour et de la méfiance, typique du réalisateur Fritz Lang.

"Some people have been unkind. If I say I want to grow as an actress, they look at my figure. If I say I want to develop, to learn my craft, they laugh. Somehow they don't expect me to be serious about my work."
**Marilyn Monroe**

„Manche Leute waren nicht nett. Wenn ich ihnen sagte, ich wollte mich schauspielerisch verbessern, dann schauten sie auf meine Figur. Wenn ich sagte, ich wollte mich entwickeln, mein Handwerk lernen, dann lachten sie. Irgendwie erwarteten sie nicht, dass ich meine Arbeit ernstnahm."
**Marilyn Monroe**

« Certaines personnes n'étaient pas très gentilles avec moi. Si je leur disais que je voulais devenir une meilleure actrice, ils jaugeaient ma silhouette. Si je disais que je voulais développer mon talent, apprendre mon métier, ils riaient. D'une certaine manière, ils ne s'attendaient pas à ce que prenne mon travail au sérieux. »
**Marilyn Monroe**

**ON THE SET OF 'CLASH BY NIGHT' (1952)**
With camera operator Fred Bentley. /
Mit Kameramann Fred Bentley. / Avec le chef
opérateur Fred Bentley.

**STILL FROM 'WE'RE NOT MARRIED' (1952)**
Is she the new "Mrs." Mississippi, or just "Miss" Mississippi? / Ist sie die neue „Mrs." Mississippi oder bloß „Miss" Mississippi? / « Est-ce qu'elle est la nouvelle "Mme" Mississippi ou juste "Miss" Mississippi ? »

**STILL FROM 'WE'RE NOT MARRIED' (1952)**
This farce hinges on a set of marriage licenses, suddenly rendered invalid. / Dieses Lustspiel dreht sich um eine Reihe von Eheschließungen, die sich nachträglich als ungültig erweisen. / Cette farce s'articule autour d'une série de mariages brusquement invalidés.

**STILL FROM 'WE'RE NOT MARRIED' (1952)**
A perpetual beauty contestant, her child now born
out of wedlock. / Eine häufige Teilnehmerin an
Schönheitswettbewerben mit einem unehelichen
Kind. / Perpétuelle reine de beauté, avec son enfant
né hors mariage.

**STILL FROM 'WE'RE NOT MARRIED' (1952)**
With her perplexed former husband (David Wayne). /
Mit ihrem verblüfften Ex-Ehemann (David Wayne). /
Dans les bras de son ex-mari perplexe (David Wayne).

**STILL FROM 'DON'T BOTHER TO KNOCK' (1952)**
Elisha Cook, Jr. has been knocked senseless by
Marilyn. / Eddie (Elisha Cook jr.) wurde von Nell
(Monroe) bewusstlos geschlagen. / Elisha Cook Jr
assommé par Marilyn.

PAGES 66/67
**STILL FROM 'DON'T BOTHER TO KNOCK' (1952)**
Battling Lurene Tuttle, mother of little Donna
Corcoran. / Im Kampf mit Ruth (Lurene Tuttle), der
Mutter der kleinen Bunny (Donna Corcoran). / À la
lutte avec Lurene Tuttle, la mère de la petite Donna
Corcoran.

**PORTRAIT FOR 'DON'T BOTHER TO KNOCK'
(1952)**
Despite the come-hither title, serious film noir co-
starring Richard Widmark. / Trotz des flapsigen Titels
handelt es sich um einen ernsthaften Film noir mit
Richard Widmark in einer weiteren Hauptrolle. /
Malgré le titre racoleur, un vrai film noir avec Richard
Widmark.

## ON THE SET OF 'DON'T BOTHER TO KNOCK' (1952)

Taking a cue from director Roy Ward Baker. / Hier nimmt sie eine Anweisung von Regisseur Roy Ward Baker entgegen. / Écoutant les recommandations du réalisateur Roy Ward Baker.

## STILL FROM 'DON'T BOTHER TO KNOCK' (1952)

As Nell Forbes, gone mad with grief over the loss of her fiancé. / Als Nell Forbes, eine junge Frau, die von ihrer Trauer um ihren Verlobten in den Wahnsinn getrieben wurde. / Dans le rôle de Nell Forbes, une jeune femme folle de désespoir suite à la disparition de son fiancé.

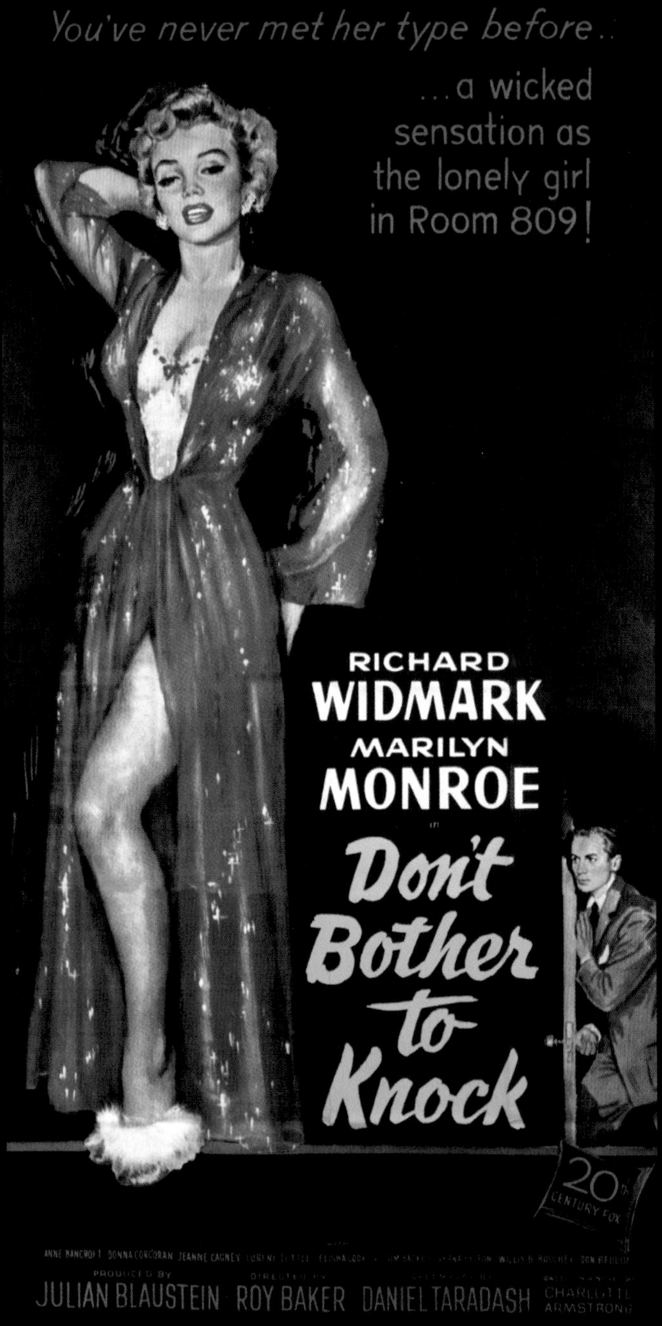
You've never met her type before...
...a wicked sensation as the lonely girl in Room 809!
RICHARD
WIDMARK
MARILYN
MONROE
in
Don't Bother to Knock
20th CENTURY FOX
ANNE BANCROFT DONNA CORCORAN JEANNE CAGNEY
PRODUCED BY
JULIAN BLAUSTEIN
ROY BAKER
DANIEL TARADASH
ARMSTRONG

ADVERT FOR 'DON'T BOTHER TO KNOCK'
(1952)

POSTER FOR 'DON'T BOTHER TO KNOCK'
(1952)

**STILL FROM 'MONKEY BUSINESS' (1952)**
After drinking a 'youth serum,' Grant goes literally wild
over her. / Nachdem er ein „Jugendserum" getrunken
hat, ist Dr. Fulton (Grant) buchstäblich wild auf sie. /
Après avoir avalé un « sérum de jeunesse », Grant se
déchaîne.

**STILL FROM 'MONKEY BUSINESS' (1952)**
Cary Grant is a scientist oblivious to her charms, at
first. / Cary Grant spielt einen Wissenschaftler, der
ihre Reize zunächst nicht wahrzunehmen scheint. /
Cary Grant dans le rôle d'un scientifique indifférent
à ses charmes, au début.

**ON THE SET OF 'MONKEY BUSINESS' (1952)**
Howard Hawks, a great master of farce (seated, center), was their director. / Howard Hawks, ein großer Meister des Lustspiels (sitzend, Mitte), führte Regie. / Sous la direction de Howard Hawks, grand maître de la farce (assis, au centre).

**STILL FROM 'MONKEY BUSINESS' (1952)**
This was the only time she teamed with Grant, but the result was delightful. / Dieser Film war ihr einziger mit Grant, aber das Ergebnis war köstlich. / Ce film fut l'occasion de son unique collaboration avec Grant. Le résultat est fort agréable.

**STILL FROM 'O. HENRY'S FULL HOUSE' (1952)**
Charles Laughton thinks he is being seductive, but
Marilyn is strictly business. / Soapy (Charles Laughton)
hält sich für verführerisch, aber für das Strichmädchen
(Marilyn) ist alles nur Geschäft. / Charles Laughton
pense la séduire, mais Marilyn n'a que le travail en
tête.

**PORTRAIT (c. 1952)**
The more she took charge of her own career, the more
elegant her poses. / Je mehr sie ihre Karriere selbst in
die Hand nahm, desto eleganter wurden ihre Posen. /
Plus elle prenait en charge sa propre carrière, plus ses
poses étaient élégantes.

PAGE 78
**PORTRAIT FOR 'NIAGARA' (1953)**
Married to her career, honeymooning amid mist. / Mit
der Karriere verheiratet, im Nebel flitternd. / Mariée à
sa carrière, en lune de miel avec la brume.

# FOXY LADY

## SEXY LADY

## SEX-SYMBOL

**STILL FROM 'NIAGARA' (1953)**
Alone in bed. Are we truly expected to believe her
husband used the other bed? / Allein im Bett. Soll der
Zuschauer wirklich glauben, dass der Ehemann das
andere Bett benutzte? / Seule au lit. Est-on vraiment
censé croire que son mari dormait dans un autre lit ?

**PORTRAIT FOR 'NIAGARA' (1953)**
Her onscreen persona accelerated her to stardom
with this role. / Mit dieser Rolle machte sie ihre Lein-
wandfigur endgültig zum Star. / Son personnage à
l'écran conquiert le statut de vedette avec ce rôle.

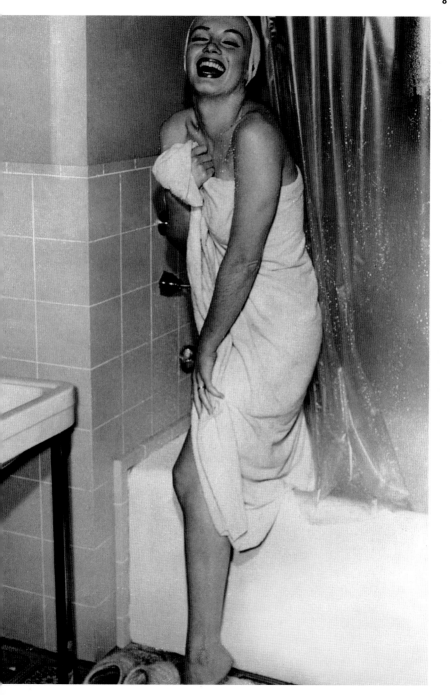

**STILL FROM 'NIAGARA' (1953)**
Canoodling with Richard Allen, free while her
husband is missing, or dead. / Während Roses
Ehemann verschollen oder tot ist, kann sie
ungehindert mit Patrick (Richard Allen)
knutschen. / Faisant des mamours à Richard Allen,
libre, alors que son mari est porté disparu, ou mort.

**STILL FROM 'NIAGARA' (1953)**
Joseph Cotten is her husband, returned 'from the
dead,' and enraged. / Joseph Cotten spielt ihren
Ehemann, der „von den Toten zurückkehrt" und eine
Stinkwut hat. / Joseph Cotten est son mari, revenu
« d'entre les morts », et fou de rage.

PAGES 84/85
**PORTRAIT FOR 'NIAGARA' (1953)**

"No one ever told me I was pretty when I was a little girl. All little girls should be told they're pretty, even if they aren't."
Marilyn Monroe

„Als ich ein kleines Mädchen war, sagte mir niemand, dass ich hübsch sei. Man sollte allen kleinen Mädchen sagen, dass sie hübsch sind, selbst wenn es nicht stimmt."
Marilyn Monroe

**PORTRAIT FOR 'GENTLEMEN PREFER BLONDES' (1953)**
Her signature role: an entertainer seeking love, aglow with desire and desirability. / Ihre typische Rolle – als Unterhalterin auf der Suche nach der Liebe, glühend vor Begierde und Begehrlichkeit. / Son rôle fétiche : une artiste de music-hall en quête d'amour, rayonnante de désir et de charme.

« Personne ne m'a jamais dit que j'étais jolie quand j'étais une petite fille. Toutes les petites filles devraient s'entendre dire qu'elles sont jolies, même si ce n'est pas vrai. »
Marilyn Monroe

**STILL FROM 'GENTLEMEN PREFER BLONDES' (1953)**

Tommy Noonan is the wealthy heir-apparent, under her spell. / Tommy Noonan spielt den reichen Erben, der ihr verfällt. / Tommy Noonan joue le riche héritier présomptif qu'elle a envoûté.

**PORTRAIT FOR 'GENTLEMEN PREFER BLONDES' (1953)**

Thriving under the direction of Howard Hawks, in step with pal Jane Russell. / Unter der Regie von Howard Hawks blühte sie auf – im Einklang mit Jane Russell. / En pleine forme sous la houlette de Howard Hawks, dans un pas de deux amical avec Jane Russell.

**STILL FROM 'GENTLEMEN PREFER BLONDES'
(1953)**
"Diamonds are a girl's best friend," she sings, amid a chorus of obliging donors. / Vor einer Reihe williger Geber singt sie „Diamonds Are a Girl's Best Friend" („Diamanten sind die besten Freunde einer Frau"). / « Les diamants sont les meilleurs amis des femmes », chante-t-elle au milieu d'un chœur de serviables donateurs.

**STILL FROM 'GENTLEMEN PREFER BLONDES'
(1953)**
Here we have the iconic Marilyn, on top of the world at last. / Hier haben wir die Ikone Marilyn, die endlich den Gipfel ihres Ruhmes erklommen hat. / Voici l'icône Marilyn aux anges, enfin.

**PUBLICITY FOR 'GENTLEMEN PREFER BLONDES' (1953)**
Marilyn and Jane Russell make their mark in the sidewalk at the famed Grauman's Chinese Theatre. / Marilyn Monroe und Jane Russell hinterlassen ihre Abdrücke im Innenhof des berühmten „Grauman's Chinese Theatre". / Marilyn et Jane Russell laissent leurs empreintes devant le célèbre Grauman's Chinese Theatre.

**STILL FROM 'GENTLEMEN PREFER BLONDES' (1953)**
Charles Coburn flirtatiously examines her delicate hands: there is a boy under the blanket and her head is sticking out of a porthole. / Charles Coburn untersucht flirtend ihre zarten Hände: Unter der Decke steckt allerdings ein Junge, während ihr Kopf aus einem Bullauge hervorschaut. / Charles Coburn examine ses mains délicates en séducteur : un jeune garçon est en fait caché sous la couverture et Marilyn sort la tête d'un hublot.

**ON SET (1951)**
Careful grooming and preparations were necessary
for every shot. / Sorgfältige Vorbereitungen waren für
jede Aufnahme notwendig. / Chaque prise nécessite
un maquillage et des préparatifs minutieux.

**ON SET (c. 1957)**
No time is wasted: a serious discussion while waiting
for her hair to be done. / Es wurde keine Zeit
verschwendet: eine ernsthafte Diskussion, während
gleichzeitig ihre Frisur gerichtet wird. / En coulisse,
pas une minute à perdre : une discussion sérieuse pendant la séance de coiffure.

**PORTRAIT FOR 'HOW TO MARRY
A MILLIONAIRE' (1953)**
Cavorting with anonymous extras, strengthening her
screen persona as a gold-digger. / Beim Herumtollen
mit unbekannten Statisten unterstrich sie ihre
Leinwandpersona der „Goldgräberin", die es nur auf
das Geld der Männer abgesehen hat. / S'amusant avec
des figurants anonymes, elle renforce son alter ego
cinématographique sous les traits d'une « chercheuse
d'or ».

**PORTRAIT FOR 'HOW TO MARRY
A MILLIONAIRE' (1953)**
She reels in her catch. / Beim Einholen ihres „Fangs". /
Marilyn en train de ferrer sa proie.

**STILL FROM 'HOW TO MARRY
A MILLIONAIRE' (1953)**

With Alex D'Arcy, in a dream sequence. "What's my motivation," she asked director Jean Negulesco. He replied: "You're blind as a bat without your glasses." / Mit Alex D'Arcy in einer Traumsequenz. „Was ist meine Motivation?", fragte sie Regisseur Jean Negulesco. Er antwortete ihr: „Ohne deine Brille bist du blind wie ein Maulwurf." / Avec Alex D'Arcy, dans une séquence onirique. « Quelle est ma motivation ? », demanda-t-elle au réalisateur Jean Negulesco. Il lui répondit : « Sans tes lunettes, tu es aveugle comme une chauve-souris. »

*"If I play a stupid girl, and ask a stupid question, I've got to follow it through. What am I supposed to do, look intelligent?"*
**Marilyn Monroe**

### STILL FROM 'HOW TO MARRY A MILLIONAIRE' (1953)

Her eyeglasses are indeed the very emblem of sexiness, as she cuddles with David Wayne. This was the last of four pictures she made with Wayne – more than any other actor. / Ihre Brille ist tatsächlich ein Symbol ihrer erotischen Ausstrahlung, wenn sie sich an David Wayne kuschelt. Dies war der letzte ihrer vier Filme mit Wayne – mehr als mit jedem anderen Schauspieler. / Ses lunettes sont effectivement d'un érotisme achevé dans cette scène où elle câline David Wayne. Ce film est le dernier qu'elle tourne aux côtés de Wayne – qui a joué avec elle dans quatre films, plus que tout autre acteur.

*„Wenn ich ein doofes Mädchen spiele und eine doofe Frage stelle, dann muss ich dabei bleiben. Was soll ich denn tun – intelligent ausschauen?"*
Marilyn Monroe

*« Si je joue une fille idiote qui pose une question idiote, il faut bien que j'aille jusqu'au bout. Qu'est-ce que je suis censée faire, avoir l'air intelligent ? »*
Marilyn Monroe

**PORTRAIT FOR 'HOW TO MARRY
A MILLIONAIRE' (1953)**
The press hoped for jealous battles with her co-stars,
Lauren Bacall and Betty Grable, but the three got
along just fine. / Die Presse lauerte darauf, dass sie
sich mit ihren Kolleginnen Lauren Bacall und Betty
Grable eifersüchtig bekriegte, aber die drei kamen gut
miteinander aus. / La presse espérait assister à des
pugilats entre elle et ses partenaires féminines Lauren
Bacall et Betty Grable, mais les trois femmes
s'entendirent à merveille.

**ON THE SET OF 'HOW TO MARRY
A MILLIONAIRE' (1953)**
Within weeks of opening, the film grossed five times
its original budget. / Innerhalb weniger Wochen hatte
der Film das Fünffache seines ursprünglichen Budgets
eingespielt. / Dans les quelques semaines qui suivirent
son arrivée à l'écran, le film rapporta cinq fois son
budget de départ.

*"I'm not interested in money, I just want to be wonderful."*
**Marilyn Monroe**

„*Geld interessiert mich nicht. Ich möchte nur wunderbar sein.*"
**Marilyn Monroe**

« *L'argent ne m'intéresse pas, je veux juste être merveilleuse.* »
**Marilyn Monroe**

**STILL FROM 'RIVER OF NO RETURN' (1954)**
As a saloon singer, in a film she grew to detest. /
Als Saloonsängerin in einem Film, den sie später verabscheute. / En chanteuse de saloon, dans un film qu'elle en vint à haïr.

**STILL FROM 'RIVER OF NO RETURN' (1954)**
Robert Mitchum (left) is a man fresh out of prison,
trying to rebuild his life with a small son he barely
knows (Tommy Rettig, right). / Robert Mitchum (links)
spielt einen Mann, der gerade aus dem Gefängnis
entlassen wurde und versucht, mit seinem kleinen
Sohn (Tommy Rettig, rechts), den er kaum kennt,
ein neues Leben zu beginnen. / Robert Mitchum
(à gauche) vient de sortir de prison et tente de
reconstruire sa vie avec son jeune fils qu'il connaît à
peine (Tommy Rettig, à droite).

**STILL FROM 'RIVER OF NO RETURN' (1954)**
Outlaws, indians and raw nature all menace the trio, as the saloon girl is swept along in this father and son drama. / Das Mädchen aus dem Saloon wird in dieses Vater/Sohn-Drama hineingezogen, und das Trio wird von Verbrechern, Indianern und der unwirtlichen Natur gleichermaßen bedroht. / Hors-la-loi, indiens et paysages hostiles menacent le trio alors que la fille de saloon est embarquée dans ce tête-à-tête dramatique entre père et fils.

*"There is a need for aloneness which I don't think most people realize for an actor. It's almost having certain kinds of secrets for yourself that you'll let the whole world in on only for a moment, when you're acting."*
**Marilyn Monroe**

*„Es gibt für einen Schauspieler ein Bedürfnis nach Einsamkeit, das den meisten Menschen, glaube ich, nicht bewusst ist. Wenn man schauspielert, dann ist es fast, als habe man bestimmte Geheimnisse, die man einen Augenblick lang der ganzen Welt offenbart."*
**Marilyn Monroe**

*« Il y a un besoin d'être seul dont la plupart des gens n'imaginent pas l'importance pour un acteur. C'est presque comme si vous aviez en vous certains secrets et que vous laissiez le monde entier les entrevoir l'espace d'un instant, lorsque vous jouez. »*
**Marilyn Monroe**

**STILL FROM 'RIVER OF NO RETURN' (1954)**
Marilyn later dismissed it as, "A grade Z cowboy movie in which the acting finished second to the scenery and the CinemaScope process." / Marilyn tat den Film später ab als „Cowboyfilm von vorn bis hinten, in dem die Schauspielerei nach der Landschaft und dem Cinemascope-Verfahren nur zweitrangig war." / Plus tard, Marilyn reniera ce « western de série Z dans lequel le jeu des acteurs compte moins que les paysages et la technique du cinémascope ».

**STILL FROM 'RIVER OF NO RETURN' (1954)**
Director Otto Preminger insisted that the actors
perform their own stunts. This certainly makes for
more dynamic and involving action sequences. /
Regisseur Otto Preminger bestand darauf, dass die
Schauspieler ihre eigenen Stunts machten. Dadurch
wirken die Action-Sequenzen sicherlich dynamischer
und packender. / Le réalisateur Otto Preminger insista
pour que les acteurs fassent leurs propres cascades.
Une telle exigence rend assurément les scènes
d'action plus dynamiques et réalistes.

**STILL FROM 'RIVER OF NO RETURN' (1954)**
One stunt went awry, and nearly took Marilyn with it toppling her into the rapids of Canada's Athabasca river, and spraining her ankle. / Einer der Stunts ging um ein Haar schief und riss Marilyn beinahe in die Stromschnellen des Athabasca-Flusses in Kanada. Dabei verstauchte sie sich den Knöchel. / Une des cascades tourna mal et Marilyn se foula la cheville en tombant dans les rapides du fleuve Athabasca, au Canada.

**ON THE SET OF 'RIVER OF NO RETURN' (1954)**
Keeping that sprained ankle well elevated. /
Der verstauchte Fuß musste hochgehalten werden. /
Comment maintenir cette cheville foulée surélevée ?

**ON THE SET OF 'RIVER OF NO RETURN' (1954)**
As she suffered, so she made director Otto Preminger
(right) suffer. Both kept smiling. / Regisseur Otto
Preminger (rechts) leidet mit. Trotzdem konnten sich
beide noch ein Lächeln abringen. / Tant qu'elle souffre, le réalisateur Otto Preminger (à droite) souffre
aussi. Ils n'en perdent pas pour autant le sourire.

POSTER FOR 'THERE'S NO BUSINESS LIKE
SHOW BUSINESS' (1954)

STILL FROM 'THERE'S NO BUSINESS LIKE
SHOW BUSINESS' (1954)
Between Donald O'Connor and Mitzi
Gaynor. / Zwischen Donald O'Connor und Mitzi
Gaynor. / Entre Donald O'Connor et Mitzi Gaynor.

**STILL FROM 'THERE'S NO BUSINESS LIKE SHOW BUSINESS' (1954)**
Singing and dancing in the red-hot African number, 'Heatwave.' / Singend und tanzend in der siedend heißen Afrikanummer „Heatwave" („Hitzewelle"). / En train de danser et de chanter dans un numéro africain torride intitulé « Vague de chaleur ».

**ON THE SET OF 'THERE'S NO BUSINESS LIKE SHOW BUSINESS' (1954)**
Catching her breath and chatting with composer Irving Berlin. / Verschnaufen und Plaudern mit dem Komponisten Irving Berlin. / Reprenant son souffle en discutant avec le compositeur Irving Berlin.

**STILL FROM 'THERE'S NO BUSINESS LIKE SHOW BUSINESS' (1954)**

"Hardest job we ever had," said co-writer Henry Ephron. "All the scenes were clichés." / „Der härteste Auftrag, den wir je hatten", stöhnte Mitautor Henry Ephron. „Sämtliche Szenen waren Klischees." / « Le boulot le plus difficile qu'on ait jamais eu », confia le coscénariste Henry Ephron. « Toutes les scènes étaient des clichés. »

**ON THE SET OF 'THERE'S NO BUSINESS LIKE SHOW BUSINESS' (1954)**

Marilyn only accepted the role to win fresh contract concessions from the studio. / Marilyn nahm die Rolle nur an, um dem Studio neue vertragliche Zugeständnisse abringen zu können. / Marilyn n'accepta le rôle que pour signer un nouveau contrat plus avantageux avec le studio.

*"People had a habit of looking at me as if I were some kind of mirror instead of a person. They didn't see me, they saw their own lewd thoughts, then they white-masked themselves by calling me the lewd one."*

**Marilyn Monroe**

*„Die Leute hatten die Gewohnheit, mich anzuschauen, als sei ich eine Art Spiegel und keine Person. Sie sahen nicht mich, sondern ihre eigenen lüsternen Gedanken, und dann spielten sie selbst die Unschuldigen, indem sie mich als lüstern bezeichneten."*

**Marilyn Monroe**

*« Les gens avaient cette habitude de me regarder comme si j'étais une espèce de miroir et non une personne. Ils ne me voyaient pas, ils voyaient leurs propres pensées obscènes, et ensuite ils s'aveuglaient et m'accusaient, moi, d'obscénité. »*

**Marilyn Monroe**

## ON THE SET OF 'THE SEVEN YEAR ITCH' (1955)

Probably the most famous single image of Marilyn Monroe. William Trevilla designed this aerodynamically pleated, ecru summer dress and halter top. / Wahrscheinlich die berühmteste Einzelaufnahme von Marilyn Monroe. William Trevilla entwarf dieses strömungsgünstig gefaltete ekrüfarbene Sommerkleid mit rückenlosem Oberteil. / Sans doute le cliché le plus célèbre de Marilyn Monroe. Cette robe d'été écrue à dos nu et au plissé aérodynamique a été conçue par William Trevilla.

PAGES 120 & 121

## ON THE SET OF 'THE SEVEN YEAR ITCH' (1955)

Co-star Tom Ewell (page 120, at left) and director Billy Wilder (page 121, at left) do their part as throngs of fans watch. The moment was later restaged and reshot in Hollywood. / Kollege Tom Ewell (Seite 120, links) und Regisseur Billy Wilder (Seite 121, links) tun ihre Arbeit, während eine Ansammlung von Fans zuschaut. Die Szene wurde später in Hollywood nachgedreht. / Son partenaire Tom Ewell (page 120, à gauche) et le réalisateur Billy Wilder (page 121, à gauche) font leur métier sous le regard d'une foule d'admirateurs. Cette scène fut ensuite tournée à nouveau à Hollywood.

**STILL FROM 'THE SEVEN YEAR ITCH' (1955)**
Tom Ewell is a married man feeling the call of the wild
after seven years of faithful husbandry. Marilyn is The
Girl, his nameless upstairs neighbor. / Tom Ewell spielt
einen verheirateten Mann, der nach sieben Jahren
ehelicher Treue den Ruf der Wildnis vernimmt.
Marilyn spielt „das Mädchen", seine namenlose
Nachbarin, die im Stockwerk über ihm wohnt. / Tom
Ewell est un homme marié qui ressent l'appel de la
nature après sept années de fidélité conjugale. Marilyn
joue La Fille, sa voisine anonyme du dessus.

*"Most men become more of what they are around
her: a phony becomes more phony, a confused
man becomes more confused, a retiring man more
retiring."*
Arthur Miller

**STILL FROM 'THE SEVEN YEAR ITCH' (1955)**
A steamy duet of 'Chopsticks' on the piano leads to an unromantic tumble. Writer George Axelrod explained, "I could never think of a name for Marilyn's character that seemed exactly right." / Ein feuchtheißer Vierhänder auf dem Flügel endet mit einem ganz unromantischen Sturz. Autor George Axelrod erklärte: „Ich konnte mir nie einen Namen für Marilyns Figur ausdenken, der genau zu passen schien." / Un charmant duo à quatre mains au piano provoque une culbute peu romantique. L'auteur, George Axelrod, expliqua : « Je n'ai jamais réussi à trouver un prénom qui convienne exactement au personnage de Marilyn. »

*„Die meisten Männer werden in ihrer Gegenwart noch mehr das, was sie ohnehin schon sind: Ein Blender wird noch unechter, ein Verwirrter noch verwirrter, ein Verschlossener noch verschlossener."*
Arthur Miller

*« À son contact, la plupart des hommes deviennent encore plus ce qu'ils sont déjà : un charlatan devient encore plus charlatan, un homme confus devient plus confus, un homme réservé plus réservé encore. »*
Arthur Miller

**STILL FROM 'THE SEVEN YEAR ITCH' (1955)**
The film's action spans a single, very hot summer night
in New York City, and The Girl stays cool by chilling her
panties in a refrigerator. / Während einer heißen
Sommernacht in New York City verschafft sich „das
Mädchen" Kühlung, indem es seine Schlüpfer im
Kühlschrank lagert. / L'action du film dure une nuit, au
cours d'un été new-yorkais caniculaire, et La Fille reste
au frais en mettant ses dessous au réfrigérateur.

**PAGES 126/127**
**PORTRAIT FOR 'THE SEVEN YEAR ITCH' (1955)**
This was Marilyn's last film for 20th Century-Fox
under straitjacket terms, for little money. / Dies war
Marilyns letzter Film für 20th Century-Fox – für wenig
Geld und dafür mit vielen Auflagen und Zwängen. /
Ce fut le dernier film que Marilyn tourna avec la
20th Century-Fox selon des termes contraignants et
peu rémunérateurs.

**STILL FROM 'THE SEVEN YEAR ITCH' (1955)**
Angelically sexy, and utterly innocent of her effect on
the likes of Tom Ewell. / Engelsgleich und sexy und
sich ihrer Wirkung auf Männer wie Tom Ewell völlig
unbewusst. / Angélique et sexy, totalement
inconsciente de l'effet qu'elle a sur Tom Ewell et
ses semblables.

**STILL FROM 'THE SEVEN YEAR ITCH' (1955)**
Tom Ewell's everyman leads a richly colored fantasy
life. Here is how the 'Chopsticks' scene would have
climaxed, if he had his way. / Tom Ewells Jedermann
führt in seiner Phantasie ein aufregendes Leben.
So hätte die Szene am Flügel geendet, wenn alles nach
seiner Vorstellung gelaufen wäre. / Monsieur Tout-le-
Monde incarné par Tom Ewell se laisse aller aux
fantasmes les plus colorés. Voilà comment se serait
terminée la scène du duo au piano s'il avait su y faire.

*"I'm a failure as a woman. My men expect so much
of me, because of the image they've made of me
and that I've made of myself, as a sex symbol. Men
expect so much, and I can't live up to it."*
**Marilyn Monroe**

**STILL FROM 'THE SEVEN YEAR ITCH' (1955)**
Fantasies aside, he gets his desired kiss in a sweet, oddly chaste way, as The Girl (who makes her living promoting toothpaste) demonstrates her "freshness of breath." / Phantasie hin oder her – er bekommt seinen Kuss auf eine süße und seltsam keusche Art, als ihm das Mädchen (das seinen Lebensunterhalt durch Zahnpastawerbung verdient) seinen „frischen Atem" demonstriert. / Fantasmes mis à part, il reçoit bien le baiser tant convoité, de façon douce et curieusement chaste, lorsque La Fille (qui gagne sa vie en faisant de la publicité pour du dentifrice) lui fait sentir « la fraîcheur de son haleine ».

„Als Frau bin ich ein Versager. Meine Männer erwarten so viel von mir, aufgrund des Bildes, das sie sich von mir als Sexsymbol gemacht haben und das ich von mir gemacht habe. Männer erwarten so viel, und ich kann diese Erwartungen nicht erfüllen."
**Marilyn Monroe**

« En tant que femme, je suis un échec. Mes hommes attendent tant de moi, à cause de mon image et de ce qu'ils ont fait de moi et de ce que j'ai fait de moi-même, en tant que sex-symbol. Les hommes attendent tant de choses et je ne peux pas être à la hauteur. »
**Marilyn Monroe**

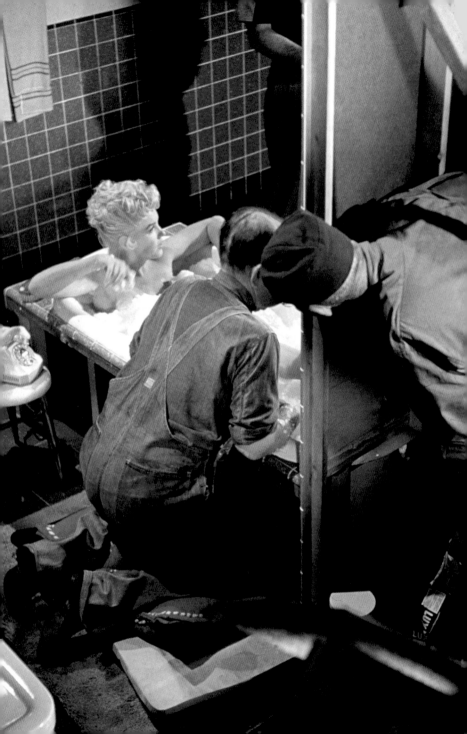

### STILL FROM 'THE SEVEN YEAR ITCH' (1955)

Director Billy Wilder observed, "She was never vulgar in a role that could have become vulgar. Somehow you always felt good when you saw her onscreen." / Regisseur Billy Wilder stellte fest: „Sie war nie vulgär in einer Rolle, die vulgär hätte werden können. Irgendwie fühlte man sich immer wohl, wenn man sie auf der Leinwand sah.“ / Le réalisateur Billy Wilder fit remarquer : « Elle n'était jamais vulgaire dans un rôle qui aurait pu le devenir. Je ne sais comment, vous vous sentiez bien lorsque vous la voyiez à l'écran. »

### ON THE SET OF 'THE SEVEN YEAR ITCH' (1955)

A more paranoid fantasy: that The Girl, trapped by her big toe in his bathtub, will make their flirtation public. / Eine etwas paranoidere Phantasie: Das Mädchen, das mit seinem großen Zeh in seiner Badewanne feststeckt, wird ihren kleinen Flirt an die Öffentlichkeit bringen. / Un fantasme plus paranoïaque : La Fille coince son gros orteil dans le siphon de la baignoire de son partenaire, révélant leur flirt au reste du monde.

PAGE 132

### PORTRAIT (1955)

Marilyn prepares to enter the prestigious Actors Studio to study Method acting. / Marilyn bereitet sich darauf vor, dem angesehenen „Actors Studio“ beizutreten, um das „Method Acting“ zu erlernen. / Marilyn s'apprête à entrer au prestigieux Actors Studio pour apprendre la « Méthode ».

# VULNERABLE

## VERLETZLICH

## VULNÉRABLE

**STILL FROM 'BUS STOP' (1956)**
Arguably her finest performance, in a wonderful role written by William Inge, in which a drifter with a past very much like her own is confronted, and confused, by the sincere love a lonely cowboy (Don Murray) expresses for her. / Möglicherweise ihre beste Schauspielleistung zeigt sie in einer wunderbaren, von William Inge geschriebenen Rolle als zielloses Mädchen mit einer ähnlichen Vergangenheit wie Marilyn selbst, das verwirrt ist von der aufrichtigen Liebe eines einsamen Cowboys (Don Murray). / Sans doute sa plus belle performance d'actrice, dans le merveilleux rôle – écrit par William Inge – d'une vagabonde dont le passé ressemble beaucoup au sien, confrontée à l'amour sincère d'un cow-boy solitaire (Don Murray), et dévastée.

*"In Hollywood a girl's virtue is much less important than her hairdo. You're judged by how you look, not by what you are. Hollywood's a place where they'll pay you a thousand dollars for a kiss, and fifty cents for your soul. I know, because I turned down the first offer often enough and held out for the fifty."*
**Marilyn Monroe**

*„In Hollywood ist die Tugend eines Mädchens viel weniger wichtig als seine Frisur. Man wird danach beurteilt, wie man aussieht, nicht wer man ist. Hollywood ist ein Ort, wo man dir tausend Dollar für einen Kuss zahlt und fünfzig Cent für deine Seele. Ich weiß es, weil ich das erste Angebot oft genug abgelehnt und auf den fünfzig bestanden habe."*
**Marilyn Monroe**

**STILL FROM 'BUS STOP' (1956)**
Director Joshua Logan was a disciple of 'method'
pioneer Konstantin Stanislavski, and so worked well
with Marilyn, but to her fury cut a soul-searching
monologue she was convinced would have won her an
Oscar. / Regisseur Joshua Logan war ein Schüler
Konstantin Stanislavskis, der das „Method Acting"
mitbegründet hatte. Er arbeitete daher gut mit
Marilyn zusammen, doch zu ihrer großen Verärgerung
schnitt er einen tiefgründigen Monolog aus dem Film
heraus, mit dem sie nach eigener Überzeugung einen
„Oscar" gewonnen hätte. / Le réalisateur Joshua
Logan était un disciple du pionnier de la « Méthode »,
Konstantin Stanislavski, et sa collaboration avec
Marilyn se passa bien, mais, à sa grande colère,
il coupa au montage un monologue introspectif dont
elle était convaincue qu'il lui aurait valu un oscar.

« À Hollywood, la vertu d'une fille compte bien
moins que sa coiffure. On vous juge sur votre
apparence, pas sur ce que vous êtes. Hollywood
est un endroit où on est prêt à vous payer mille
dollars pour un baiser et cinquante cents pour
votre âme. Je le sais, parce que j'ai refusé bien
assez souvent la première offre et insisté pour
obtenir les cinquante cents. »
**Marilyn Monroe**

WARNER BROS. present

# Laurence Olivier
## and
# Marilyn Monroe

in

# The Prince and the Showgirl

TECHNICOLOR

A Screenplay by TERENCE RATTIGAN

with

SYBIL THORNDIKE
RICHARD WATTIS
JEREMY SPENSER

Music Composed by RICHARD ADDINSELL
Music Directed by MUIR MATHIESON

Produced and Directed by
LAURENCE OLIVIER

**PORTRAIT FOR 'THE PRINCE AND THE SHOWGIRL' (1957)**
This was the only film ever produced by Marilyn Monroe Productions. Alas for her ambition, director Laurence Olivier's first bit of guidance for her was: "Just be sexy." / Dies war der einzige Film, den Marilyn Monroe Productions je produzierte. Trotz ihres gewaltigen Ehrgeizes gab ihr Regisseur Laurence Olivier als Erstes den Rat: „Sei einfach sexy." / Le seul film jamais produit par la Marilyn Monroe Productions. Hélas! le réalisateur Laurence Olivier lui octroie pour tout conseil un laconique : « Contente-toi d'être sexy. »

**ADVERT FOR 'THE PRINCE AND THE SHOWGIRL' (1957)**

**STILL FROM 'SOME LIKE IT HOT' (1959)**
As Sugar Kane Kowalczyk in what has proved her most
popular film. / Als Sugar Kane Kowalczyk in dem Film,
der zu ihrem populärsten wurde. / Dans le rôle de
Sugar Kane Kowalczyk, dans son film le plus populaire.

**STILL FROM 'SOME LIKE IT HOT' (1959)**
Having fun, singing with an all-girl 1920s band. Her
lifelong inner anguish is beginning to show, even in her
smile. / Es macht ihr Spaß, mit einer Mädchenband aus
den 1920er Jahren zu singen, aber selbst in ihrem
Lächeln deutet sich nun ihre lebenslange seelische
Qual an. / S'amusant lors d'un tour de chant avec un
groupe de jazz des années 1920 uniquement composé
de femmes. L'angoisse qui la rongea toute sa vie
commence à apparaître, même dans son sourire.

**ON THE SET OF 'SOME LIKE IT HOT' (1959)**
"Sugar Kane was the weakest part in the picture,"
recalled director Billy Wilder, "so we solved that with
the strongest possible casting." / „Sugar Kane war die
schwächste Rolle in dem Film", erinnert sich Regisseur
Billy Wilder, „also besetzten wir sie so stark wie
möglich." / « Sugar Kane était le rôle le plus faible du
film, se souvenait Billy Wilder, alors nous avons résolu
le problème en le confiant à l'actrice la plus forte
possible. »

**STILL FROM 'SOME LIKE IT HOT' (1959)**
Marilyn was miserable, and made her co-workers
equally so with her chronic lateness. Billy Wilder
would later laugh bitterly, "We were mid-flight and
there was a nut on the plane." / Marilyn ging es
miserabel. Billy Wilder scherzte später verbittert:
„Wir waren mitten im Flug und hatten eine Bekloppte
an Bord." / Marilyn était mal en point. Plus tard, Billy
Wilder en rira amèrement : « Nous étions en plein ciel
et il y avait une cinglée à bord. »

"She was our angel, the sweet angel of sex."
Norman Mailer

„Sie war unser Engel, der süße Engel des Sex."
Norman Mailer

« Elle était notre ange, le doux ange du sexe. »
Norman Mailer

**STILL FROM 'SOME LIKE IT HOT' (1959)**
She might have said no to the part, but her playwright
husband Arthur Miller greatly admired the script by
Wilder and I.A.L. Diamond, and assured her it was a
sure-fire winner. / Sie hätte die Rolle ablehnen
können, aber ihr Ehemann, der Dramatiker Arthur
Miller, hegte große Bewunderung für das Drehbuch
von Wilder und I. A. L. Diamond und versicherte ihr,
der Film werde garantiert ein Erfolg. / Elle faillit
refuser le rôle, mais son dramaturge de mari, Arthur
Miller, admirait beaucoup le scénario écrit par Wilder
et I. A. L. Diamond et la convainquit qu'il serait un
succès assuré.

PAGES 144 & 145
**ON THE SET OF & STILL FROM 'SOME LIKE IT HOT' (1959)**
As is true of so many of her best films, Marilyn was
given an opportunity to sing. / Wie in vielen ihrer
besten Filme bekam Marilyn auch hier die Gelegenheit
zu einer Gesangseinlage. / Comme dans la plupart de
ses meilleurs films, Marilyn a l'occasion d'y chanter.

PAGES 146/147
**STILL FROM 'SOME LIKE IT HOT' (1959)**
Tripped by Tony Curtis, who later declared, "kissing
Marilyn was like kissing Hitler." / Von Tony Curtis zum
Stolpern gebracht, der später sagte: „Marilyn zu
küssen war wie Hitler zu küssen." / Crochetée par
Tony Curtis, qui déclarera plus tard : « Embrasser
Marilyn, c'était comme embrasser Hitler. »

R-348-9

R-348-5

R-348-

10

6

2

7

3

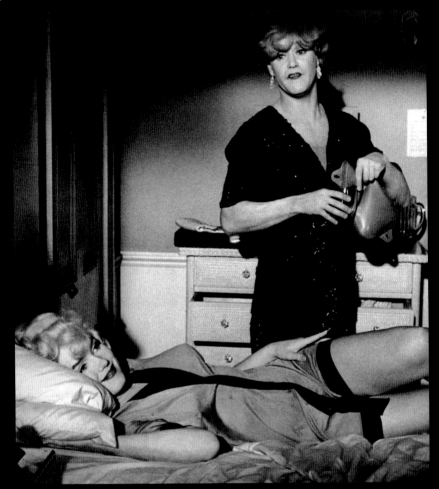

**STILL FROM 'SOME LIKE IT HOT' (1959)**
In bed, "thinking nice thoughts" as Jack Lemmon stands by, in drag. / Im Bett mit „netten Gedanken", während Jack Lemmon in Frauenkleidern zuschaut. / Au lit, « en train de penser à de jolies choses » aux côtés de Jack Lemmon, debout, travesti.

**STILL FROM 'SOME LIKE IT HOT' (1959)**
Marilyn protested that the film was being shot in black & white, but director Billy Wilder assured her that color would have destroyed the illusion that Tony Curtis and Jack Lemmon were successfully passing themselves off as women. / Marilyn protestierte dagegen, dass der Film in Schwarzweiß gedreht wurde, doch Regisseur Billy Wilder versicherte ihr, dass Farbe die Illusion zerstört hätte, Tony Curtis und Jack Lemmon könnten sich erfolgreich als Frauen ausgeben. / Marilyn critiqua la décision de tourner le film en noir et blanc, mais Billy Wilder lui assura que la couleur aurait détruit la crédibilité de Tony Curtis et Jack Lemmon travestis en femmes.

**STILL FROM 'SOME LIKE IT HOT' (1959)**
Tony Curtis (right), an excellent mimic, got to fulfill a boyhood hero-worship of Cary Grant by performing a long sequence in Grant's voice and trademark diction. / Tony Curtis (rechts), ein ausgezeichneter Imitator, konnte sich einen alten Jugendtraum erfüllen, als er in einer langen Sequenz den von ihm sehr bewunderten Cary Grant in dessen charakteristischer Stimme und Sprechweise nachahmen durfte. / Tony Curtis (à droite), excellent imitateur, réalise un rêve de petit garçon en mimant la voix et le débit caractéristiques de son héros Cary Grant au cours d'une longue séquence.

**STILL FROM 'SOME LIKE IT HOT' (1959)**
British critic Kenneth Tynan observed that the seduction scenes are particularly erotic, not because sex is shown, but because throughout, we're free to feel that 'Anything can happen.' / Der britische Kritiker Kenneth Tynan stellte fest, dass die Verführungsszenen nicht durch das Zeigen des Geschlechtsaktes besonders erotisch wirkten, sondern weil der Zuschauer durchweg das Gefühl hatte, alles sei möglich. / Le critique britannique Kenneth Tynan fit observer que les scènes de séduction étaient particulièrement érotiques, non pas parce que le sexe y était montré, mais parce que, tout du long, nous étions libres de penser que « tout [peut] arriver ».

**STILL FROM 'LET'S MAKE LOVE' (1960)**
Marilyn owed 20th Century-Fox a picture, and the result (despite this lively interlude) was a tedious dud. / Marilyn schuldete 20th Century-Fox noch einen Film, und das Ergebnis war (trotz dieses lebhaften Zwischenspiels) ein langweiliger Rohrkrepierer. / Marilyn devait un film à la 20th Century-Fox. Résultat : un navet ennuyeux – malgré cet interlude enlevé.

**STILL FROM 'LET'S MAKE LOVE' (1960)**
Cuddling Frankie Vaughan. Arthur Miller lent an uncredited hand to the script, "But we were beating a dead horse." / Beim Schmusen mit Frankie Vaughan. Arthur Miller half ungenannt beim Drehbuch nach, aber „wir prügelten auf ein Pferd ein, das schon tot war". / Câline avec Frankie Vaughan. Arthur Miller participa discrètement à l'écriture du script, mais, confia-t-il, « nous cravachions un cheval déjà mort ».

**STILL FROM 'LET'S MAKE LOVE' (1960)**
Marilyn fought for Yves Montand in the lead, won, and came to regret it when he boasted to the press that they were lovers. / Marilyn kämpfte darum, dass Yves Montand die Hauptrolle bekam, und bereute es dann, als er der Presse mitteilte, die beiden seien ein Liebespaar. / Marilyn insista pour qu'Yves Montand soit son partenaire mais le regretta plus tard lorsqu'il annonça à la presse qu'ils étaient amants.

**STILL FROM 'LET'S MAKE LOVE' (1960)**
"The worst part I ever had to play," she said later. "It wasn't even a part." / „Die schlimmste Rolle, die ich je spielen musste", sagte sie später. „Es war nicht mal eine Rolle." / « Le pire rôle que j'aie jamais eu à jouer », avouera-t-elle. « Ce n'était même pas un rôle. »

**STILL FROM 'LET'S MAKE LOVE' (1960)**
Montand plays a reclusive billionaire modeled on
American tycoon Howard Hughes. / Montand spielt
einen eigenbrötlerischen Milliardär nach dem Vorbild
des amerikanischen Tycoons Howard Hughes. /
Montand joue un milliardaire solitaire inspiré du
magnat américain Howard Hughes.

**STILL FROM 'LET'S MAKE LOVE' (1960)**
Marilyn plays an entertainer for whom the billionaire
falls when he tries to block a movie based on his life. /
Marilyn spielt eine Unterhalterin, in die sich der
Milliardär verliebt, als er einen Film über sein Leben zu
verhindern versucht. / Marilyn en artiste de music-hall
dont le milliardaire tombe amoureux alors qu'il essaie
d'empêcher la réalisation d'un film sur sa vie.

**STILL FROM 'LET'S MAKE LOVE' (1960)**
Vladimir Nabokov witnessed Marilyn's mistreatment
by Montand at a party, and vengefully caricatured the
actor in his novel 'Ada.' / Vladimir Nabokov wurde
Zeuge, wie Marilyn auf einer Party von Montand
schlecht behandelt wurde, und rächte sie, indem er
den Schauspieler in seinem Roman *Ada* karikierte. /
Vladimir Nabokov fut témoin de la manière dont
Montand avait traité Marilyn au cours d'une soirée
mondaine et la vengea en caricaturant l'acteur dans
son roman *Ada*.

**STILL FROM 'LET'S MAKE LOVE' (1960)**
A snapshot between takes captures her still
vital essence: lost yet hopeful, all at once. /
Ein Schnappschuss, der zwischen zwei Einstellungen
entstand, fängt ihr ganzes Naturell ein: verloren und
doch hoffnungsvoll, alles zugleich. / Ce cliché saisi
entre deux prises révèle son essence même,
encore palpitante : perdue mais pleine d'espoir,
tout ensemble.

"I'm trying to become an artist, and to be true, and sometimes I feel I'm on the verge of craziness, I'm just trying to get the truest part of myself out, and it's very hard. There are times when I think, 'All I have to be is true.' But sometimes it doesn't come out so easily. I always have this secret feeling that I'm really a fake or something, a phony."
**Marilyn Monroe**

„Ich versuche, eine Künstlerin zu werden und wahrhaftig zu sein, und manchmal fühle ich mich am Rande des Wahnsinns. Ich versuche nur, das Wahrhaftigste an mir herauszubringen, und es ist sehr schwer. Manchmal denke ich: ‚Ich muss nur wahrhaftig sein.' Aber manchmal kommt das nicht so einfach heraus. Ich habe insgeheim immer dieses Gefühl, dass ich in Wirklichkeit ein Schwindler bin oder etwas in dieser Art, ein Blender."
**Marilyn Monroe**

« J'essaie de devenir une artiste et d'être sincère, et parfois j'ai la sensation d'être au bord de la folie, j'essaie juste de faire sortir de moi la part qui est la plus vraie, et c'est très dur. Parfois je me dis : "Il me suffit d'être sincère." Mais parfois ce n'est pas si facile. J'ai toujours cette intime sensation que je ne suis en fait qu'un faux, une espèce d'imposteur. »
**Marilyn Monroe**

PAGES 162 & 163
**PORTRAITS FOR 'THE MISFITS' (1961)**
As a child and orphan, Marilyn often fantasized Clark Gable was her father. / Als Kind und Waise stellte sich Marilyn oft vor, Clark Gable sei ihr Vater. / Lorsqu'elle était enfant et orpheline, Marilyn s'imaginait souvent que Clark Gable était son père.

PAGES 164/165
**STILL FROM 'THE MISFITS' (1961)**
Marilyn was devastated by the news of Gable's death soon after filming ended. / Marilyn war am Boden zerstört, als sie von Gables Tod kurz nach Abschluss der Dreharbeiten erfuhr. / Marilyn fut terrassée par la mort de Gable, peu après la fin du tournage.

**PORTRAIT FOR 'THE MISFITS' (1961)**
Circling her, clockwise from top: Arthur Miller, John Huston, Clark Gable, Montgomery Clift, and Eli Wallach. / Es umgeben sie, im Uhrzeigersinn von oben: Arthur Miller, John Huston, Clark Gable, Montgomery Clift und Eli Wallach. / Autour d'elle, de gauche à droite en partant du haut : Arthur Miller, John Huston, Clark Gable, Montgomery Clift et Eli Wallach.

**STILL FROM 'THE MISFITS' (1961)**
A consummate player, thriving in a circle of equals. / Eine vollendete Schauspielerin unter ihresgleichen. / Une actrice parfaite, s'épanouissant parmi ses semblables.

**STILL FROM 'THE MISFITS' (1961)**
Arthur Miller created Roslyn Tabor – complex, adrift, loving, conscientious – to highlight Marilyn's gifts, and to echo her private nature, and deepest angers. / Arthur Miller erfand Roslyn Tabor – vielschichtig, ziellos, liebevoll, gewissenhaft –, um Marilyns positive Eigenschaften hervorzuheben und ihr zutiefst zorniges privates Ich widerzuspiegeln. / Arthur Miller crée Roslyn Tabor – complexe, à la dérive, tendre, consciencieuse – pour mettre en lumière les dons de Marilyn et pour donner à voir sa nature intime, et sa colère la plus profonde.

PAGES 168/169
**STILL FROM 'THE MISFITS' (1961)**
"You're the only person I've ever met who's more screwed up than me," she told Montgomery Clift. / „Du bist der einzige Mensch, den ich je kennengelernt habe, der noch verkorkster ist als ich", sagte sie zu Montgomery Clift. / « Tu es la seule personne que j'aie jamais rencontrée qui soit plus dingue que moi », confiera-t-elle à Montgomery Clift.

**STILL FROM 'SOMETHING'S GOT TO GIVE'
(1962)**
Ellen (Marilyn), lost for years on a desert island, has
come back to rejoin her family. A light-hearted premise,
but it was the first time Marilyn was cast as a wife and
mother. / Ellen (Marilyn), jahrelang auf einer einsamen
Insel verschollen, ist zu ihrer Familie zurückgekehrt.
Die Grundidee war eigentlich unbeschwert, aber
Marilyn spielte hier zum ersten Mal eine Ehefrau und
Mutter. / Ellen (Marilyn), qui est restée échouée
pendant des années sur une île déserte, revient pour
réunir sa famille. L'intrigue semble légère, mais c'est la
première fois que Marilyn joue le rôle d'une épouse et
d'une mère.

**STILL FROM 'SOMETHING'S GOT TO GIVE'
(1962)**
A promising role as a woman come back from
the dead. The film was never completed. / Eine
vielversprechende Rolle als Frau, die von den Toten
auferstanden ist. Der Film wurde nie fertiggestellt. /
Un rôle prometteur de femme revenue d'entre les
morts. Le film est resté inachevé.

**STILL FROM 'SOMETHING'S GOT TO GIVE'
(1962)**
Dean Martin (center) played her husband, Cyd
Charisse (right) the woman he married when believing
Marilyn dead. / Dean Martin (Mitte) spielte ihren
Ehemann, Cyd Charisse (rechts) die Frau, die er
heiratete, weil er seine erste Frau für tot hielt. /
Dean Martin (au centre) jouait son mari, Cyd Charisse
(à droite) la femme qu'il a épousée après avoir cru
Marilyn morte.

*"I knew I belonged to the public and to the world,
not because I was talented or even beautiful, but
because I never had belonged to anything or
anyone else."*
Marilyn Monroe

„Ich wusste, dass ich der Öffentlichkeit und der Welt gehörte – nicht, weil ich talentiert oder gar schön war, sondern weil ich nie etwas oder jemand anderem gehört hatte."
**Marilyn Monroe**

« Je savais que j'appartenais au public et au monde, non parce que j'étais douée ou même belle, mais parce que je n'avais jamais appartenu à quiconque ou quoi que ce soit d'autre. »
**Marilyn Monroe**

### STILL FROM 'SOMETHING'S GOT TO GIVE' (1962)

Her death left this film unfinished (it was later remade as 'Move Over, Darling,' with Doris Day), but such footage as survives shows Marilyn in sweet form, interacting easily with her onscreen children. / Durch ihren Tod wurde der Film nie fertiggestellt (es gab später ein Remake mit Doris Day unter dem Titel *Move Over, Darling* [*Eine zuviel im Bett*]), aber das erhaltene Material zeigt Marilyn ganz in ihrem Element, wie sie locker mit ihren Filmkindern umgeht. / Sa mort laisse le film inachevé (il sera refait sous le titre *Move Over, Darling* avec Doris Day), mais de telles images montrent une Marilyn toute en sensualité, très à l'aise avec ses enfants acteurs.

**STILL FROM 'SOMETHING'S GOT TO GIVE'
(1962)**
A last, luminous glimpse of Marilyn, swimming naked
and inviting the world to join her. / Ein letzter
leuchtender Blick auf Marilyn, die nackt schwimmt
und die Welt einlädt, es ihr gleichzutun. / Une dernière
et éblouissante vision de Marilyn : nageant nue,
et semblant inviter le monde entier à la rejoindre.

**STILL FROM 'SOMETHING'S GOT TO GIVE'
(1962)**
Still a beauty, though her chronic insomnia and
addiction to sleeping pills took its toll. / Noch
immer eine Schönheit, wenngleich ihre chronische
Schlaflosigkeit und ihre Abhängigkeit von
Schlaftabletten Spuren hinterließen. / Toujours en
beauté, malgré ses insomnies chroniques et sa
consommation excessive de somnifères.

**JFK'S BIRTHDAY GALA (1962)**
"Happy Birthday" was never ever sung more
seductively than on this night, in honor of JFK. /
„Happy Birthday" wurde niemals verführerischer
gesungen als an diesem Abend zu Ehren von JFK. /
« Happy Birthday » ne fut jamais chanté avec plus de
sensualité que ce soir-là, en l'honneur du Président
J. F. Kennedy.

**JFK'S BIRTHDAY GALA (1962)**
President John F. Kennedy (center) receives this
tribute alertly, coolly, much the way he later
contemplated Soviet missiles in Cuba. / Präsident JFK
(Mitte) nimmt diesen Tribut genauso gelassen
entgegen wie später die Stationierung sowjetischer
Raketen auf Kuba. / Le Président (au centre) reçoit
l'hommage avec réserve, un peu comme il accueillera
plus tard la présence de missiles soviétiques à Cuba.

PAGE 178
**ARTHUR MILLER & MARILYN MONROE (1957)**
Their wedding day. The New York Post proclaimed:
'Egghead Weds Hourglass.' / Ihr Hochzeitstag. Die *New
York Post* titelte: „Eierkopf heiratet Eieruhr." / Le jour
de leur mariage, le *New York Post* proclamait : « La
grosse tête épouse le sablier. »

# 3

# CHRONOLOGY

## CHRONOLOGIE

## CHRONOLOGIE

## MARILYN MONROE (1928)

Norma Jean, age two, with her mother (beside parasol). / Norma Jean im Alter von zwei Jahren mit ihrer Mutter (neben dem Sonnenschirm). / Norma Jean, à l'âge de deux ans, avec sa mère (à côté de l'ombrelle).

**1 June 1926** Norma Jean Mortenson [Marilyn Monroe] is born in Hollywood, California, USA.

**1926–1942** Her mother Gladys Monroe cannot care for her. Martin Mortenson, her father of record on the birth certificate, is likely not the actual father and does not take an interest. MM lives in foster homes and orphanages.

**19 June 1942** Two weeks after her 16th birthday, MM escapes her 'legal orphan' status by marrying a friend, James Dougherty.

## September 1946–December 1948

Divorces James Dougherty. Works as a model and then as a contract player for both Fox and Columbia Pictures.

**1949–1950** Johnny Hyde, a top agent at the William Morris agency, brilliantly guides her early career and becomes her lover. Hyde persuades John Huston to cast her in The Asphalt Jungle, the film which effectively launches her career.

**1951** 20th Century-Fox upgrades her latest 6-month contract into a 7-year deal.

**1953** Protesting low wages and poor career management by Fox, rebels and suffers suspensions by the studio.

**January 1954–October 1955** Marries and divorces baseball player Joe DiMaggio.

**7 January 1955** MM and Milton Greene form Marilyn Monroe Productions, which begins a year-long battle with Fox. Meanwhile, she studies acting with Lee Strasberg.

**4 January 1956** Fox agrees to MM's terms. Her career turns a major corner for the better.

**12 February 1956** Performs bar room scene from Anna Christie by Eugene O'Neill at the Actors Studio in New York.

**29 June 1956** Marries Arthur Miller.

1956–1957 Two pregnancies end in miscarriage.

4 August–6 November 1958 Whilst filming *Some Like It Hot*, is so repeatedly late for work that it becomes part of her public image.

17 December 1958 Third miscarriage.

June 1960 Begins seeing psychiatrist Ralph Greenson.

November 1960 Has a nervous breakdown.

20 January 1961 Divorces Arthur Miller.

May 1962 Sings 'Happy Birthday' to JFK at Madison Square Garden.

June 1962 20th Century-Fox uses Marilyn's appearance at the JFK gala as evidence of a breach of contract, and shuts down her nearly complete new film, *Something's Got to Give*.

1 August 1962 After a month of negotiation, Fox and MM sign a renewed contract at an even higher salary. *Something's Got to Give* is slated to restart immediately.

**MARRIAGE TO JAMES DOUGHERTY (1942)**
Their wedding day. / Ihr Hochzeitstag. / Le jour de son premier mariage, à l'âge de 16 ans.

4 August 1962 Accounts of MM's last day abound in gossip, rumor, speculation and conspiracy theory. The hard facts, sorted most thoroughly and persuasively by biographer Donald Spoto, indicate MM suffered a fatal, but accidental, overdose of barbiturates when a sedative-laced enema was administered to her in the early evening, without taking proper account of how many pills she'd already ingested in the course of the long day.

5 August 1962 At 3:50 am, MM is officially declared dead.

# CHRONOLOGIE

**1. Juni 1926** Norma Jean Mortenson [Marilyn Monroe] wird in Hollywood (Kalifornien, USA) geboren.

**1926–1942** Ihre Mutter, Gladys Monroe, kann nicht für sie sorgen. Martin Mortenson, in ihrer Geburtsurkunde als Vater benannt, ist wahrscheinlich nicht ihr leiblicher Vater und zeigt auch kein Interesse an ihr. Norma Jean beginnt im frühesten Kindesalter eine Odyssee durch Waisenhäuser und Pflegefamilien.

**19. Juni 1942** Zwei Wochen nach Vollendung ihres 16. Lebensjahres entflieht Norma Jean ihrem Status als „juristische Waise", indem sie ihren Freund James Dougherty heiratet.

**September 1946–Dezember 1948** Sie lässt sich von James Dougherty scheiden und sucht Arbeit als Model. Sie macht auch Probeaufnahmen für Filme und wird von Fox und Columbia Pictures unter Vertrag genommen.

**1949–1950** Johnny Hyde, Top-Agent bei der William-Morris-Agentur, erkennt ihre Qualitäten, geleitet sie auf vorbildliche Weise bei den ersten Schritten auf der Karriereleiter und wird privat zu ihrem Liebhaber. Hyde hat sie es zu verdanken, dass ihr John Huston eine Rolle in *The Asphalt Jungle* (*Asphalt-Dschungel*) gibt, dem eigentlichen Beginn ihrer Karriere.

**1951** 20th Century-Fox verlängert ihren ursprünglichen Halbjahresvertrag auf sieben Jahre.

**1953** Als sie gegen Niedriglöhne und schlechtes Karrieremanagement bei Fox protestiert, wird sie vom Studio auf Eis gelegt.

**Januar 1954–Oktober 1955** Sie heiratet die Baseball-Legende Joe DiMaggio und lässt sich 19 Monate später scheiden.

**7. Januar 1955** MM und Milton Greene gründen die Marilyn Monroe Productions. Damit beginnt ein jahrelanger Kampf mit Fox.

**4. Januar 1956** Fox stimmt den Forderungen von MM zu. Damit erlebt ihre Karriere einen deutlichen Aufschwung.

**12. Februar 1956** Sie spielt im „Actors Studio" in New York die Barszene aus Eugene O'Neills *Anna Christie*.

**29. Juni 1956** Sie heiratet Arthur Miller.

**1956–1957** Zwei Schwangerschaften enden mit Fehlgeburten.

**4. August–6. November 1958** Während der Dreharbeiten zu *Manche mögen's heiß* erscheint sie so oft zu spät zur Arbeit, dass die Unpünktlichkeit zu einem Teil ihres Images in der Öffentlichkeit wird.

**17. Dezember 1958** Dritte Fehlgeburt.

**Juni 1960** Sie beginnt eine Therapie bei dem Psychiater Ralph Greenson.

**November 1960** Sie erleidet einen Nervenzusammenbruch.

**20. Januar 1961** Sie lässt sich von Arthur Miller scheiden.

**19. Mai 1962** Sie singt „Happy Birthday" für JFK im Madison Square Garden.

**Juni 1962** Die 20th Century-Fox wertet Marilyns Auftritt während der JFK-Gala als Vertragsbruch und stoppt ihren fast vollendeten neuen Film, *Something's Got to Give* (*Marilyn – Ihr letzter Film*).

**1. August 1962** Nach einmonatigen Verhandlungen schließen Fox und MM einen neuen Vertrag mit einer noch höheren Gage ab. Die Dreharbeiten zu *Something's Got to Give* sollen sofort wiederaufgenommen werden.

**5. August 1962** Um 3:50 Uhr wird MM amtlich für tot erklärt. Die Berichte über den letzten Tag im Leben von Marilyn Monroe stecken voller Gerüchte, Klatsch, Spekulation und Verschwörungstheorien. Die Fakten deuten darauf hin, dass MM an einer tödlichen, jedoch unbeabsichtigt eingenommenen Überdosis an Barbituraten starb.

**IN KOREA (1954)**
Singing to the US forces in Korea. Skintight gown, no underwear, sub-zero cold: "For the first time in my life I felt no fear of anything," she later recalled. "I felt only happy." / Beim Singen für die US-Streitkräfte in Korea. Hautenges Kleid, keine Unterwäsche, Temperaturen unter Null: „Zum ersten Mal in meinem Leben spürte ich keinerlei Angst", erinnerte sie sich später, „ich war einfach nur glücklich." / Chantant pour les troupes américaines en Corée. Robe collante, pas de sous-vêtements, un froid polaire : « Pour la première fois de ma vie, je n'avais plus peur de rien », se souvint-elle. « Je me sentais juste heureuse. »

# CHRONOLOGIE

**1ᵉʳ juin 1926** Norma Jean Mortenson (Marilyn Monroe) voit le jour à Hollywood, en Californie.

**1926–1942** Sa mère, Gladys Monroe, ne peut subvenir à ses besoins et Martin Mortenson – son père légitime (c'est son nom qui apparaît sur le certificat de naissance) mais vraisemblablement pas son père biologique – se désintéresse de son sort. Marilyn est placée dès son plus jeune âge et passe son enfance entre orphelinats et familles d'accueil.

**19 juin 1942** Deux semaines après son 16ᵉ anniversaire, la jeune Marilyn échappe à son statut d'« orpheline officielle » en épousant son ami James Dougherty.

**Septembre 1946–décembre 1948** Divorce de James Dougherty. Cherche des emplois de mannequin, fait des essais pour le cinéma, est prise sous contrat à la fois chez Fox et Columbia Pictures.

**1949–1950** Johnny Hyde, célèbre figure de l'agence William Morris, orchestre avec talent sa carrière naissante et devient son amant. Hyde convainc John Huston de l'engager pour *Quand la ville dort*, le film qui va réellement la lancer.

**1951** La 20th Century-Fox transforme son dernier contrat de 6 mois en contrat de 7 ans.

**1953** Parce qu'elle se rebelle contre les salaires misérables et les médiocres opportunités de carrière que lui procure la Fox, elle est suspendue par les studios.

**Janvier 1954–octobre 1955** Épouse le joueur de base-ball Joe DiMaggio et s'en sépare en octobre.

**7 janvier 1955** Marilyn Monroe et Milton Greene créent la maison Marilyn Monroe Productions. C'est le début d'une bataille d'un an avec la Fox. Mais Marilyn ne reste pas inactive et étudie le jeu d'acteur avec le maître Lee Strasberg.

## PORTRAIT (1953)

In her golden gown from 'How to Marry a Millionaire,' the flaming embodiment of Elton John's song 'Candle in the Wind.' / In ihrem goldenen Abendkleid aus *Wie angelt man sich einen Millionär?* als flammende Verkörperung von Elton Johns Lied „Candle in the Wind". / Dans la robe qu'elle portait pour *Comment épouser un millionaire*. Incarnation flamboyante de la chanson d'Elton John *Candle in the Wind*.

**4 janvier 1956** La Fox accepte les conditions de Marilyn Monroe. Sa carrière prend un nouveau virage, des plus bénéfiques.

**12 février 1956** Présente une scène entière d'*Anna Christie* d'Eugene O'Neill à l'Actors Studio de New York.

**29 juin 1956** Épouse Arthur Miller.

**1956–1957** Tombe enceinte deux fois et fait deux fausses couches.

**4 août–6 novembre 1958** Tourne *Certains l'aiment chaud*; ses retards sur le plateau sont si fréquents qu'ils deviennent un trait de son image publique.

**17 décembre 1958** Troisième fausse couche.

**Juin 1960** Commence ses séances avec le psychiatre Ralph Greenson.

**Novembre 1960** Fait une dépression nerveuse.

**20 janvier 1961** Divorce d'Arthur Miller.

**19 mai 1962** Chante « Happy Birthday » en l'honneur du Président Kennedy à Madison Square Garden.

**Juin 1962** La 20th Century-Fox prend prétexte de l'apparition de Marilyn au gala pour l'accuser de rupture de contrat et arrête le tournage de son plus récent film, presque achevé, *Something's Got to Give*.

**1ᵉʳ août 1962** Après un mois de négociation, la Fox et Marilyn Monroe signent ensemble un nouveau contrat, à un salaire plus élevé encore. Le tournage de *Something's Got to Give* doit reprendre d'un jour à l'autre.

**4 août 1962** La dernière journée de Marilyn Monroe a alimenté ragots, rumeurs, spéculations et théories du complot. Les faits objectifs, présentés de façon rigoureuse et convaincante par son biographe Donald Spoto, indiquent que Marilyn Monroe a succombé à une overdose fatale mais accidentelle de barbituriques après qu'un lavement aux sédatifs lui a été administré en début de soirée, sans que soit pris en compte le nombre de pilules qu'elle avait déjà ingérées pendant toute cette longue journée.

**5 août 1962** À 3h50 du matin, le décès de Marilyn Monroe est officiellement annoncé.

# 4

# FILMOGRAPHY

## FILMOGRAFIE

## FILMOGRAPHIE

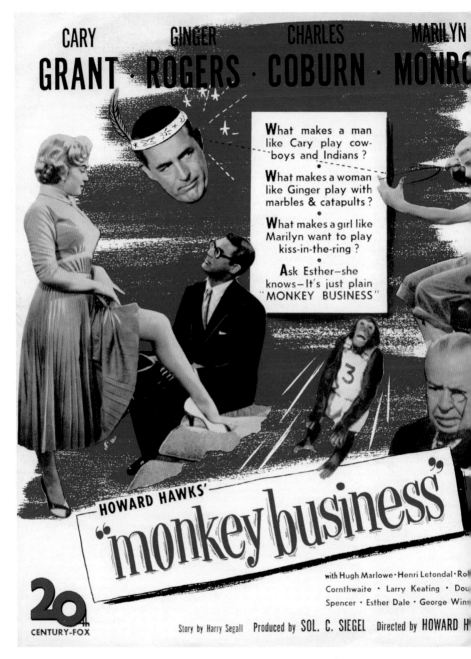

Dangerous Years (1947)

Scudda Hoo! Scudda Hay! (1948)

Ladies of the Chorus/Ich tanze in dein Herz/
La Reine du music-hall (1948)

Love Happy/Love Happy/La Pêche au trésor
(1950)

A Ticket to Tomahawk/A Ticket to
Tomahawk/Le Petit Train du Far West (1950)

The Asphalt Jungle/Asphalt-Dschungel/
Quand la ville dort (1950)

All about Eve/Alles über Eva/Ève (1950)

The Fireball/Rollschuhfieber/The Fireball (1950)

Right Cross/Der einsame Champion/Right
Cross (1950)

Home Town Story (1951)

As Young as You Feel/Alter schützt vor
Torheit nicht/Rendez-moi ma femme (1951)

Love Nest/Love Nest/Nid d'amour (1951)

Let's Make It Legal/Let's Make It Legal/Chéri,
divorçons (1951)

Clash by Night/Vor dem neuen Tag/Le
Démon s'éveille la nuit (1952)

We're Not Married/Wir sind gar nicht
verheiratet/Cinq mariages à l'essai (1952)

Don't Bother to Knock/Versuchung auf
809/Troublez-moi ce soir (1952)

Monkey Business/Liebling, ich werde
jünger/Chéri, je me sens rajeunir (1952)

O. Henry's Full House/Fünf Perlen (a. Vier
Perlen)/La Sarabande des pantins (1952)

Niagara (1953)

Gentlemen Prefer Blondes/Blondinen bevor-
zugt/Les hommes préfèrent les blondes (1953)

How to Marry a Millionaire/Wie angelt man
sich einen Millionär?/Comment épouser un
millionnaire (1953)

River of No Return/Fluß ohne Wiederkehr/La
Rivière sans retour (1954)

There's No Business Like Show Business/
Rhythmus im Blut/La Joyeuse Parade (1954)

The Seven Year Itch/Das verflixte 7. Jahr/Sept
ans de réflexion (1955)

Bus Stop/Bus Stop/Arrêt d'autobus (1956)

The Prince and the Showgirl/Der Prinz und
die Tänzerin/Le Prince et la Danseuse (1957)

Some Like It Hot/Manche mögen's
heiß/Certains l'aiment chaud (1959)

Let's Make Love/Machen wir's in Liebe/Le
Milliardaire (1960)

The Misfits/Misfits – Nicht gesellschaftsfähig/
Les Désaxés (1961)

Something's Got to Give/Marilyn – Ihr letzter
Film/Something's Got to Give (unfinished/
nicht fertiggestellt/inachevé, 1962)

# THE TIMELESS MAGIC OF
# MARILYN

# BIBLIOGRAPHY

**Churchwell, Sarah:** *The Many Lives of Marilyn Monroe.* Henry Holt, 2004.

**Conway, Michael & Ricci, Mark:** *The Films of Marilyn Monroe.* Citadel Press, 1964.

**Kazan, Elia:** *A Life.* Knopf, 1989.

**Leaming, Barbara:** *Marilyn Monroe.* Crown Publishers, 1998.

**Mailer, Norman:** *Marilyn, A Biography.* Grosset & Dunlap, 1973.

**Miller, Arthur:** *Timebends, An Autobiography.* Grove Press, 1987.

**Miller, Arthur:** *After the Fall (a play): Collected Plays of Arthur Miller.* Viking Penguin, 2004.

**Miller, Arthur:** *Finishing the Picture (a play).* Staged 2004, unpublished.

**Monroe, Marilyn:** *My Story.* (As told to writer Ben Hecht, circa 1955. Hecht's manuscript languished for years until it was resurrected, rewritten by her business partner Milton Greene, and published in the wake of the enormous success of the Mailer book.) Stein & Day, 1974.

**Reise, Randall & Hitchens, Neal:** *The Unabridged Marilyn - Her Life from A to Z.* Congdon & Weed, 1987.

**Spoto, Donald:** *Marilyn Monroe. The Biography.* HarperCollins, 1993.

**Strasberg, Susan:** *Marilyn and Me, Sisters, Rivals, Friends.* Warner Books, 1992.

**Summers, Anthony:** *Goddess - The Secret Lives of Marilyn Monroe.* Macmillan, 1985.

**Victor, Adam:** *The Marilyn Encyclopedia.* The Overlook Press, 1999.

# IMPRINT

© 2006 TASCHEN GmbH
Hohenzollernring 53, D-50672 Köln
www.taschen.com

Editor/Picture Research/Layout: Paul Duncan/Wordsmith Solutions
Editorial Coordination: Martin Holz, Cologne
Production Coordination: Nadia Najm and Horst Neuzner, Cologne
German translation: Thomas J. Kinne, Nauheim
French translation: Alice Petillot, Paris
Multilingual production: www.arnaudbriand.com, Paris
Typeface Design: Sense/Net, Andy Disl and Birgit Reber, Cologne

Printed in Italy
ISBN-13: 978-3-8228-2117-6
ISBN-10: 3-8228-2117-9

To stay informed about upcoming TASCHEN titles, please request our magazine at www.taschen.com/magazine or write to TASCHEN, Hohenzollernring 53, D-50672 Cologne, Germany, contact@taschen.com, Fax: +49-221-254919. We will be happy to send you a free copy of our magazine which is filled with information about all of our books.

All the photos in this book were supplied by The Kobal Collection.

**ENDPAPERS/VORSATZ/PAGES DE GARDE**
**PORTRAITS FOR 'THE PRINCE AND THE SHOWGIRL' (1957)**

**PAGES 2/3**
**STILL FROM 'HOW TO MARRY A MILLIONAIRE' (1953)**

**PAGE 4**
**PORTRAIT FOR 'HOW TO MARRY A MILLIONAIRE' (1953)**

**PAGE 6**
**PORTRAIT (1953)**

**PAGES 8/9**
**STILL FROM 'THE SEVEN YEAR ITCH' (1955)**